Remember Us

*A collection of memories from Hungarian
Hidden Children of the Holocaust*

Contributing Editors

Judy Abrams & Evi Blaikie

authorHOUSE®

AuthorHouse™
1663 Liberty Drive, Suite 200
Bloomington, IN 47403
www.authorhouse.com
Phone: 1-800-839-8640

First published by AuthorHouse 2/11/2010

ISBN: 978-1-4389-2915-6 (e)
ISBN: 978-1-4389-2905-7 (sc)

Printed in the United States of America
Bloomington, Indiana

This book is printed on acid-free paper.

Cover design by Kate Taylor.

Table of Contents

Remember Us

We were children small and smaller
Most of us never to grow older.
Swept away by terror of darkness
Some survived to tell the tale
Each of us in our own way.

We do not comprehend why
We were chosen to stay alive
Generations of innocents were lost
Volcanoes erupted
Consumed the unwanted.

Turbulent rivers turned red
As the world stood silently still
Witnessing the slaughter of our future
Musicians, parents, teachers and writers,
Scientists and scholars, healers and dancers

And dreamers—lost in the great void—
Beseeching us with melody interrupted.
Remember us!
In your hearts and souls,
Remember us!

Miriam Steinmetz, 2007

THE HUNGARIAN HIDDEN CHILDREN
A Manhattan, New York–based child survivor group

At the first International Conference for the Hidden Child in New York City, in 1991, a group of men and women of Hungarian origin who had, as children, survived the Holocaust by hiding, met and founded a group called the Hungarian Hidden Children, (HHC).

They met at the conference and exchanged memories. Before the Holocaust, many had lived in the same neighborhoods, attended the same schools, been taught by the same teachers, and had belonged to the same Jewish scout troops (having been excluded from the regular scouts). Once the window to their past had been cracked open, they felt that it could not be closed, and they decided to meet again.

These founding members committed themselves to six consecutive monthly meetings to decide whether there was any reason to form an association. Thus the HHC was born. For many it was the first time that they were able to talk freely about their trauma-filled childhoods with people who understood, who had had the same experiences, recognized the same catchwords, euphemisms, and spoke the same language of their childhood. Not the language they now, perhaps, spoke better, but the one they remembered speaking to their mothers and fathers when they were children. For many it was a very emotional experience.

The first two years were devoted for the most part to a form of group therapy. There were many tears shed as half-forgotten memories came tumbling out: Stories of abandonment, memories of sights and sounds that no child should ever see or hear, reliving the fear, hunger, and cold of the dreadful winter of 1944. These were the themes of the meetings of that initial healing period until it was decided that there had to be other areas of interest and topics to explore besides the past.

Eventually, programs were organized in advance. These now include discussions of videos; lectures by historians, psychoanalysts, activists; and visits to museums and summer outings.

The HHC keeps a library of films pertaining to Jewish culture, history, and the Holocaust. Occasionally a member of the group presents. Gabor Vermes, PhD, retired professor of European history at Rutgers University, will steer the group through some Jewish history (see *The Jews of Hungary: A Brief History* at the end of this book), and Susan Bendor, PhD, devoted activist and an associate professor at Yeshiva University in New York, will bring everyone up to date on the ills of the world and exhort us all to help children who are now in harm's way, as all the members of the group once themselves were.

Meetings are rotated among members who can accommodate the group, and each program is preceded by an hour of schmoozing and eating. Yearly dues are collected, including an emergency fund in case any member becomes sick and or finds him/herself in difficulty. Charitable contributions are made, along with a yearly gift to the Memorial Museum of Hungarian Speaking Jewry in Safed, Israel, which has become a special, adopted cause.

Paid up membership is around forty members. Over the years, members have come, gone, and come back again. Two original members have passed away: Dr. Magda Denes and Judith Thaler.

There was particular pride and satisfaction when a Hungarian Jew, Imre Kertész, won the Nobel Prize for Literature in 2003, especially since he wrote about his experiences as a child in Auschwitz and aimed his writing at demanding that those Hungarians who participated in the slaughter recognize their role in collaborating with the Nazi policy of the Final Solution. When some members of the Hungarian government vocally resented this award being given to a Jew, the HHC placed ads in Hungarian newspapers congratulating Imre Kertész.

Thus far, there have been four published authors within HHC:

- Gabor Vermes, PhD, author of *István Tisza: The Liberal Vision and Conservative Statecraft of a Magyar Nationalist.*
- Zahava Stessel, PhD, author of *Wine and Thorns in the Tokay Valley: Jewish Life in Hungary. A history of Abaujszánto*
- Magda Denes, PhD, (1934–1996), author of *Castles Burning: A Child's Life in War* and *In Necessity* and *Sorrow: Life and Death in an Abortion Hospital*
- Evi Blaikie, author of *Magda's Daughter: A Hidden Child's Journey Home*

The Hungarian Hidden Children have created this book so that when we are no more, our children, grandchildren, and those yet unborn can read about this tragic period in our history through the words of the children who were there.

EB

About the Stories

On the following pages, each member of the HHC recalled a particular situation, event, or series of events that was a significant episode for them during the war.

These are not the horror tales of the Holocaust, about which so many books have been written. Most of these stories are just glimpses—the sudden vision that pops into the child's mind when the word "Holocaust" in heard. Others delved into their stories more deeply, needing to explain, to understand, and perhaps to see in print, the tragic, incomprehensible events that changed their lives. Some of these stories are tragic, some absurd, some sad, some totally unexpected, but taken as a whole, they illustrate how children react to and experience war.

The Holocaust in Hungary was of a shorter duration than in other European countries, and though the devastation matched that of the rest of Europe owing to the speed and brutality that the Germans and the Hungarian Fascists had already perfected, those who remained in hiding had a greater chance of survival. Consequently, the percentage of Jewish children who survived the Holocaust is greater in Hungary than in other countries, and of those who survived, a larger percentage had surviving parents. However, the statistics are still grim. Out of a Jewish population numbering approximately 800,000, almost two thirds, 560,000, were murdered. Most died in the notorious concentration camp at Auschwitz. Many men perished in the particularly Hungarian institution called *Munkaszolgálat*, a form of forced labor battalions within the Hungarian army that Jewish men were conscripted into and from which few returned.

Most of the contributors to this book originate from Budapest. The rural areas, small towns, and the county seats were the first to be cleared of Jews by murder or deportation. Budapest was left till last, and though thousands were deported from there or shot into the Danube, the Germans and Hungarian Fascists did not succeed in gathering them all before their defeat by the Allies. Consequently, the largest number of surviving Hungarian Jews hail from Budapest.

Many of the survival stories seem "miraculous". But survival at that time, under the circumstances, could indeed be seen as such. Many still wonder about their own survival.

Memories are ephemeral and changeable. They are composites of reality as perceived by us as children and as others, the adults around us, recollected them. These versions coalesced and were further transformed, for some of us, by what we were told and retold. Thus, the facts in our stories may not always be exact; however, the emotions elicited by our experiences have remained with us. These feelings, often still raw, motivated us to write this book.*

*The stories are sprinkled with terms such as Safe Houses, Jewish Houses or Yellow Star house, Arrow Cross, March 19th, false papers, coal cellars, the Brick Factory, yellow stars, DP camp, etc, which are part of the war vocabulary but which may require explanations to those unfamiliar with those terms. Please refer to glossary at the end of the book or log onto the Holocaust glossary website at: http://fcit.usf.edu/holocaust/RESOURCE/glossary.htm

Each story is followed by a short biography and pictures of the author.

EB

Susan Bendor, Ph.D

Common Themes in the Lives of Hungarian Hidden Children

There is no question that the Holocaust traumatized child survivors in countless ways, imposing damages and challenges that were most visible and invisible, conscious and unconscious, immediate and long term, cruel and life-altering for many.

It is, however, also true that the survivors integrated their experiences into their lives in very different ways. As the stories in this book demonstrate, the Hungarian Hidden Children shared many common themes of danger, separation, hunger, displacement, and the need to be silent, hyper-vigilant, and invisible—in other words, the need not to be a child. These themes were interspersed with inspiring episodes of courage, friendship, hope, and caring that enabled them to survive.

Their experiences influenced them in very different ways, e.g. from marrying non – Jews in order to feel safe, to becoming successful business people for security, to becoming helping professionals, activists, and Holocaust educators to alleviate and prevent the suffering of others.

It is also important to note that for most child survivors, the concentration camp or hiding experience was followed by many years of emigration and immigration to various countries, always feeling like outsiders. These insecurities of never feeling "At Home" or wanted were based partly on the stigma of being the despised, persecuted Jew that pervaded their early lives, and the new stigma of the "immigrant", or to borrow Marjorie Agosin's term, of being "uncertain travelers" (from *Uncertain Travelers: Conversations with Jewish Immigrant Women*, Brandeis University Press, 1999).

A section on the common themes in the lives of Hungarian Hidden children cannot end without acknowledging the strengths, coping skills, flexibility, and resilience these children demonstrated both as children and adults in their capacities to adapt to a relentless set of difficult changes and deprivations. They developed the capacity to build a better life and forged a moral conscience that will not allow them to stand by silently in the face of human suffering.

Susan Bendor, PhD, is a member of the Hungarian Hidden Children. Her story and her biography appear in this book.

Dr. Judit Szekacs-Weisz
London, 2008

BORROWED IDENTITIES

Evi Blaikie, the editor of this haunting collection of memories talks about "borrowed identities."

The term is precise and profound. It describes a transitory state of being, a life often on the verge of life and death. The function of this temporary identity is to hide and protect, to give the self a disguise, a new shape and form, which might offer a chance to escape.

This new identity is hanging between the "me" and "not-me". It functions like a second skin. At the same time it is alien. It demands complete adaptation and concentration: The slightest mistake or confusion can cost one's life.

What an incomprehensible and nonsensical psychological task to "suspend" the person one is and to carry on as somebody else!

How can a child do this?!

The testimony of the Hungarian Hidden Children gives evidence that this is exactly what they had to do. And they did it.

They were expected to switch from one day to the next. To leave behind the familiar streets, houses, people, objects, smells, beliefs, words, and even their names—those fundamentals that they thought nobody could, or would ever try, to take away from them; perhaps being allowed to hold on to, a toy, a glove, or a pillow, to serve as a bridge in their mind between the unknown and home.

This is how they went into hiding. Most of them remaining in the same country; in many cases, the same city, surrounded by the same streets and houses where they learned the basics of the whole wide world around them: "*Trust the adults*" "*Respect your neighbors*,", and "*Believe in common sense.*"

They looked at the same sky, spoke the same language, but the elementary order of things was being lost: "*Nothing made sense…the emptiness I felt inside and outside made no sense,*" recalls one of the child survivors of the Budapest Holocaust.

This feeling reverberates in the experience of all refugees and emigrants whose continuity of being has been forcefully interrupted- but never more powerfully or full of such pain.

The majority of these children were born into safety, financial security, and culture; daughters and sons of respected and prosperous citizens of a fast developing Central-European country:

Hungary. The youngest a few months old, the oldest 14, in 1944, when their world turned irreparably off its axis.

The Germans invaded the country, and the Hungarian Arrow Cross was given unlimited power to the project of murdering the local Jewish population.

They did a good job.

An increasingly tightening net was cast around Jewish families so that they could be easily caught and destroyed. However it did not completely paralyze all of them.

People with possibilities—courage, connections, access to documents, hiding places, action plans—were mobilized and came to help, at least to save the children. In the majority of cases this was expensive—but people who helped risked their lives nevertheless.

"We hid in attics, basements, and unoccupied apartments of kind people"

"A young woman dressed in black opened the heavy gate. I had seen nuns before … but never one so near. She motioned us to enter. My stomach constricted: it felt as though I had swallowed a pebble …she smiled as she reached for my hand. By the time the latch clicked on the gate, my mother was outside, and I was locked in. I wondered if the pebble in my middle would ever dissolve."

The life-saving moment for a seven-year-old Jewish girl, who becomes from then on "Ilona Papp, a Catholic child whose parents live in the Hungarian countryside

"Our housekeeper took me to her village, pretending that I was hers, born during the years of service in the city …"

"…we were to hide in one of the giant empty crates used to store bales of paper …"

"we were now under the protection of the German SS… SS Major Kurt Becher charged twenty thousand dollars for each family…. Armed German soldiers and members of the SS guarded us against the Arrow Cross patrols, often using violence against them …"

"There were many people in the shelter, and I had to resume using my new name. We settled into the coal bin away from the others …"

"My father had a client…. she suggested that we should move in with her and provide her with financial compensation as well as favorable testimony after the war… if we survived …"

"The Swiss Red Cross covered all the expenses, but the man in charge was Gabor Sztehlo, a Lutheran pastor, who managed to save the lives of a thousand Jewish children living in thirty homes …"

Everyday encounters with madness!

Simple accounts of the incomprehensible!

They don't understand—they just cope.

They keep silent, walk, do as they are told, don't ask questions. Learn to be called by false names, prepare to play dead when shot into the Danube. Carry secret information to the resistance. They survive bestial cruelty, lose parents, siblings, and family—- and won't have *"the luxury to mourn"*.

But they will live. They are the children from the geographical center of Europe with stories that will never become past tense.

Fifty years pass before they share their memories with the community of other hidden children whose childhood has been shattered with brutal force.

Now they allow us to listen to their stories and understand: Understand that traumatic experiences of this kind can never be fully worked through or repaired. They can be survived. Among favorable conditions, life can become meaningful again. The capacity of feeling and thinking can return, and trust in human relations can be rediscovered. Children can be born, grow up to be free, and digest some of their parents' past.

The courage to revisit the underworld of Hungarian history is a statement in itself.

The stories they tell us command respect and call for reflection. They enable different generations to listen and to take possession of their own experience.

This is a crucial step toward facing individual and social history: without it, a sense of continuity and true identity cannot be reestablished and integration cannot take place.

Dr. Judit Szekacs-Weisz, bilingual psychoanalyst and psychotherapist

Dr. Szekacs was born Budapest, Hungary, where the largest part of her education took place. She was influenced by the thoughts and ideas of Ferenczi, the Balints, Hermann, and Rajka, as the integral part of a "professional mother tongue."

The experience of living and working in a totalitarian regime and the transformative years leading to the fall of the Berlin Wall sensitized her to the social and individual aspects of trauma, identity formation, and strategies of survival.

She moved to London in 1990, where now she lives and works.

With a small group of colleagues she founded the Imago East-West and the Multilingual Psychotherapy Center and organized several conferences, including the Lost Childhood and Language Exile conference in London (2001). She writes about body and mind, trauma, changing context, mother tongue, emigration, and living and working in a second country, language, and culture.

The Stories

Budapest 1941

Hungary 1944

Judy Abrams

HOW THE BEADS SAVED ME

My mother and I walked hand in hand, along "Fasor" (Tree Row), a broad boulevard in Budapest lined with flowering wild chestnut trees. Pink and white blossom clusters were set among the lush foliage, like miniature Christmas trees, showering us with their petals and creating a soft pastel carpet for our steps. It was the spring of 1944.

In the summer, round and spiky green pods would begin to weigh down the branches. They would drop to the pavement in early fall, splitting open to release glossy mahogany chestnuts. I loved to rub the smooth shells, still slightly moist as they left their prickly cocoons. I collected them by the bagful to hoard in the deep drawer of a white cabinet outside my bedroom. When they lost their sheen and began to wrinkle, like the wizened faces of old men, I no longer cared if they were thrown out, knowing that the shiny new crop of the following fall would take their place. There was going to be no chestnut harvest for me in the fall. The German army had marched into Hungary on March 19, 1944.

My mother held my hand tighter than necessary. I was seven years old and not likely to rush into the road. In any case, there weren't many cars passing by in the early afternoon. To the few pedestrians who saw us, we must have seemed inconspicuous. My pretty, dark-haired mother wore her fashionable, light gray tweed suit and held me by the hand, a little girl in a pale blue knitted dress. Two large matching blue bows attached my thick, brown braids to each other, twin butterflies' wings propelling me on along the boulevard lined with festive trees. We both carried our coats draped over our arms. It was quite warm for April, not unusual to want to walk coatless in the sun. Nobody would guess that a dangerous mission prompted this innocent act. The coats, casually turned inside out, bore the telltale yellow cloth stars that identified us as Jews. The German occupiers had ordered all Jews to wear one whenever they left their homes.

My father was active in the Zionist movement. He realized the obligatory yellow star was just the beginning of what was to happen to the Hungarian Jews. Refugees from Czechoslovakia and Poland had given the Zionists accounts of atrocities committed by the Germans in their countries. He heeded these warnings and found a way to get a genuine Catholic birth and baptismal certificate for me.

"I'm not ashamed that I'm Jewish," I had said to my parents when I first watched my mother sew the yellow stars on our coats. "I'm proud of it."

I don't remember the words my parents used to convince me that my newfound pride had to be abandoned, but I obediently folded my coat inside out as we walked along the alley of blooming chestnut trees, toward the Ursuline convent on Stefánia út.

My mother rang the outer bell on the gate of a tall, black iron railing. A young woman dressed in black opened the heavy gate. I had seen nuns before, at a distance, usually walking in pairs on the street, but never one so near. She motioned us to enter. My stomach constricted. It felt as though I had swallowed a pebble.

The patch of face visible under the stiff white band across the forehead of the nun seemed friendly. Her ears and neck were covered by a starched, white, bib-like collar to which a long, black veil was attached. Not a strand of her hair could be seen. She smiled reassuringly as she reached for my hand. The latch clicked on the gate. My mother was now outside, and I was locked in. I wondered if the pebble in my middle would ever dissolve.

Did my mother kiss me before she left? She may have said good-bye in words that ended in *"Pipikém"* (my little chicken), her favorite endearment for me in Hungarian. Did she turn to wave to me? I don't remember. I wasn't watching her anymore. A new game was beginning when she let go of my hand, leaving me on my own with the strange woman in the long, black gown. We went along a stony garden path that led to a yellow, stucco, two-story villa. My companion walked briskly. The cross attached to the long string of large beads circling her waist seemed to bounce at every step.

The interior of the house we were entering was shuttered. White sheets covered all the furniture, just like in our apartment in Budapest when we left for summer vacation by Lake Balaton or to the Mátra Mountains. Massive, draped chairs and sofas stood guard in the eerie half-light.

The young nun told me I would stay in this house for a few days, but soon I would meet other children who had already left the city to live in a beautiful house with a large garden across the Danube.

"Mother Superior is waiting to meet you." I followed her without understanding who this mother was. We found this tall nun, with a silk veil finer than my companion's, in the only bright and cheerful room of the gloomy house.

She called me Ili, short for Ilona. This was now my name, and it would replace any other that I had been called for the seven previous years of my life. I would no longer be Judit, Jutka, or Juditkám for a long time. I understood that it would be dangerous to tell people my real name. How had my parents impressed upon me the importance of this pretence? I never gave away my secret. For now, I was Ilona Papp, a Catholic child whose parents lived in the Hungarian countryside. I must have been told that the nuns and Maria would take care of me until we were together again, although I don't remember thinking about our reunion in the months that followed. In fact, I seemed not to think about my parents at all. My recently found pride in being Jewish had disappeared. I seemed to have really become Ilona Papp, a much safer identity than my own.

It was our devout Catholic friend Maria who had convinced Mother Superior to accept me as a boarder. She promised my parents that she'd visit me every month and would be responsible for me in their absence. Maria and the nuns were taking great risks by taking charge of this Ilona Papp who had been Judit Grünfeld until the moment she stepped into the convent garden. My parents sent the convent a trunk full of monogrammed linen—"my dowry"—my mother told me many years later, trying to make light of the reason for this premature marriage preparation.

I didn't cry, not even while I ate a solitary snack in the convent's large, empty kitchen, or when I was put in an adult-sized bed under an unfamiliar comforter covered in white cotton.

The next day, my education began. A short, chubby nun, whose red cheeks and cheerfulness were the features I still remember, told me the stories I would have to know in order to survive. She must have explained the identity of the silver figure on the wooden cross hanging from the beaded belts the nuns wore. She gave me a picture of Jesus as a blond, curly haired child, pointing to his glowing heart, to use as a bookmark in my new, little black prayer book. (I still have these mementoes of my Christian past.)

I was a good student, and in a few days I knew the Ave Maria and the Lord's Prayer by heart. I learned how to use the pearly white beads of my new rosary and to repeat the prayers in the correct order. I was ready to enter a new world.

I didn't protest when scissors snipped the threads that held the yellow star on my sky blue coat before a Sister and I boarded the train for the brief journey from Budapest to Pincehely. She presented our documents to the Hungarian gendarmes, a special unit distinguished by their plumed helmets and particular hostility to Jews. The two men mumbled "Honor to Jesus Christ," the standard greeting expressing respect for nuns. They looked fondly at the sweet Christian girl on her way to be schooled by the Ursulines. It was all so easy now that I no longer wore a yellow star. I had become a real Hungarian girl.

When we arrived, I saw a long, unvarnished wooden table set in the garden for an afternoon snack. A half-dozen girls and boys sat on benches next to it. A nun in a swishing black habit brought me big chunks of crusty, buttered country bread and a large mug of milky coffee. No more cocoa in my porcelain cup with the blue forget-me-nots. I was ready for the new treat until I noticed a hard, leathery layer forming on the surface of the drink. I hated the 'skin' of hot milk. Was this un-Christian? I closed my eyes and, almost choking on the slimy film, gulped down the warm liquid without pausing for breath.

I spent the spring and summer months in the sprawling mansion, surrounded by a beautiful park where I played with the other boarders, boys and girls, whom I now assume to have all been Jewish like me. I had willed myself to be Ili (the short form of Ilona) and eagerly continued the study of the questions and answers of the Catholic Catechism. I had the tools, a rosary of pearly white beads with a small silver crucifix and my little black prayer book soon bulging with pictures of saints. The previous life with my parents was relegated to a sinful past, in which we may have been responsible, even if unwittingly, for the crucifixion of Christ. I was no longer Judit Grünfeld of Budapest, but Ilona Papp of some small Hungarian town, and I played my role with enthusiasm.

By autumn, the convent proved to be less than safe. There were gruesome stories of raids by the SS and their cohorts, the Hungarian Arrow Cross, who were rumored to be breaking into the convents and monasteries where nuns and priests were reported to be hiding Jews. Sheltered from these events at the time, I only heard about them much after the war. All I knew then was that Maria had come to take me with her, and I was happy.

Maria liked to call me *bazsarózsa*, the Hungarian word for peony, a flower that blooms in time for my birthday at the end of April. She had come to Budapest from a small village, an orphan of sixteen looking for work—not too much younger than my mother. My grandmother hired the little country girl with the single blonde braid; she eventually ran her household and then my parents' after they married in 1936. Her parents died when she was a child, and when her grandparents, who had brought her up, did too, she had no close relatives left. She considered us her family. When I was born a year later, Maria took charge of me. She was the only person who could rock me to sleep with lullabies from her repertoire of Hungarian folksongs. I had become the child she would never have. By the time the Germans arrived in Hungary, she was no longer working for us, but for the Hungarian civil service. Nevertheless, she rushed to our house as soon as she could to offer her help. She wanted to do whatever was possible to save me. My parents trusted Maria to be there for me whenever I needed her in their, perhaps permanent, absence.

Maria and I took the train back to Budapest, carrying only my clothes in a small suitcase. There was no yellow star on my coat. She had a studio apartment on Naphegy (Sun Hill) in Buda. My grandmother and my aunt were already there. They had come to Maria in desperation a few months earlier. Even though they had "legitimate" false documents, the woman who had agreed to hide them (at a considerable price) had panicked one night and told them to leave her house. They had nowhere else to go. Maria didn't hesitate to take them in. We were crowded in the small apartment, but safe.

On Christmas Eve, we stood around the tree we had swathed in angel hair and shiny tinsel: my grandmother, my Aunt Marika, Maria, the neighbors she had invited—all genuine Catholics—and I. The candles at the tip of each branch cast their light on the presents piled underneath. Books and games were hard to come by in those days of war shortages, but Maria had gone shopping, and I knew that most of the gifts were for me. Christmas dinner had just finished. We sang traditional Hungarian Christmas carols. Poor *Nagyi* (my grandmother) found it impossible to utter the words, "Saint Mary, his holy mother ..." She stood erect and silent, dressed in her usual black. My Aunt Marika, a gentle, beautiful, and elegant lady, just pretended to sing. "Auntie Caretaker", the supervisor of our building, sang loud and clear, her mellow voice issuing from a generous, padded cabinet. She admired my devotion to the rosary, the prayer book, and my collection of saints.

We did not have a chance to reach the carol's jubilant chorus "Behold! Behold!" before the air raid sirens started to shriek. The deafening noise of cannons and bombs sent us all down two flights of steps to the basement, which was not really a proper bomb shelter. When we got there, I saw mattresses on old iron bed stands, jars of preserves on the shelves (including some Hungarian duck preserved in fat), and tall, brown jute sacks of flour, onions, and potatoes. The families who lived in the building had been preparing for the *Ostrom* (The Siege of Budapest). The Soviet Army was gradually approaching the capital, but the Germans and Hungarians had still not given up the city. That night, the battle began in earnest, with shelling, shooting, and bombs. From Christmas until February, we seldom emerged from the cellar while the house just collapsed over our heads.

There was no more electricity, and we lived mostly by the light of candles and petroleum lamps whose glass chimneys protected the flickering flames channeling smoke and fumes toward the exposed pipes overhead. The tenants huddled in family groups in the cellar, with little room to move around. Days were as long and dark as nights. I had my rosary to help me pass the time, and I prayed, moving the beads with my small fingers. My aunt tells me now that she and my grandmother were almost driven out of their minds watching me pray for hours on end, but they remained silent, and, as it turned out, those prayers served me well. Auntie Caretaker was moved by my devotion to the rosary, and she listened with admiration as I kept repeating my prayers day after dismal day.

January 1945 was very cold. The dirty snow of the garden was littered with spent shells, rubble, and fragments of broken glass. What had been a pretty, pastel stucco house a few weeks before was now a pile of rubble. We stood outside, a frightened collection of men, women, and me, the only child, obliged to leave the dubious safety of our shelter. A small group of young men with arrow cross armbands faced us menacingly. They were the *Nyilas*, members of the notorious Jew hunting brigade. Someone had reported there were Jews hiding in the building.

By that time, there were no trains to carry the remaining Hungarian Jews to the camps in Germany and Poland, but the Arrow Cross were enacting their own version of the Final Solution. Those suspected of being Jewish were marched to the Danube River and lined up on the banks. After several rounds fired by machine guns, they all disappeared into the icy waters. I'm not sure whether I had overheard some conversation about these executions. I did know that only a firm belief in my new faith and identity would save me from some dreadful fate. I sensed Maria's anger and the terror of my grandmother and my aunt. I remember feeling terribly alone as I stood in the dirty snow in my gray winter coat with the blue-lined hood. I felt awkward in its bulk, clumsy and vulnerable while our documents were examined one by one. My aunt and grandmother were given long, piercing stares, but my grandmother's icy blue eyes and my aunt's elegant profile allayed any suspicion. A sigh of relief when each of the papers was handed back to its owner without comment. It was my turn. "This birth certificate looks very new," one of the men said.

"Of course." My grandmother spoke with quiet authority. "In other times, we didn't have to carry around all these documents to prove who we were." One of the men looked at me too carefully and conferred with his colleagues.

"The child looks Jewish," were his fateful words.

I remember the lump of pain in the pit of my stomach as I stood very still, waiting. It was then that Auntie Caretaker's voice boomed out,

"Shame on you! This child prays all the time. She is a better Christian than you, you punk!" She remembered the long, dark hours I spent fingering my rosary and praying. Only the sounds of battle disturbed the quiet, which descended on the panic-stricken band of survivors. (I later found out that most of them were Jews in hiding.) There was a long silence, and then my papers were wordlessly handed back to my grandmother.

I was saved by the beads*.

Recently a chain of fortuitous contacts helped me get in touch with the Ursuline nuns of Hungary, who sent me photographs and information about the buildings I mention in my story and to learn the name of the Mother Superior, which was Orsolya Szudey. A few months after my stay, in June 1944, the building was bombed and completely destroyed—except for the chapel, where the nuns who had stayed behind had taken refuge.

New York 1983

Montreal 2004

10

Name: Judy Abrams (née Grünfeld Judit)

Born: Budapest 1937

Paternal Grandparents	**Maternal Grandparents**
Grandfather	**Grandfather**
Fülöp Grünfeld	Imre Kaba
B: Szenice, 1859	**B:** Unknown
D: Montreal, 1959	**D:** Budapest, 1927
Grandmother	**Grandmother**
Katarina (née Grünspann)	Annie (née Deutsch)
B: Vienna, 1865	**B:** Budapest, 1886
D: Budapest, 1945	**D:** Budapest, 1974
(January 25, of shrapnel wounds during Siege of Budapest)	
Parents	
Father	**Mother**
László Grünfeld	Renée (née Kaba)
B: Budapest, 1902	**B:** Budapest, 1910
D: Montreal, 1969	**D:** Montreal, 1984

Prewar

I was born in Budapest in 1937 to Renée (née Kaba) and László Grünfeld. My mother's maternal ancestors, the Deutsch-Müller family, can be traced back to their nineteenth century Hungarian Jewish middle class ancestors. My father's family had arrived more recently from northeastern Hungary and acquired their wealth as wine merchants. I was an only child, enrolled in a Montessori nursery school and later in grade one in the local elementary school in *Sziv utca*. Because of the German takeover of Hungary in March 1944, under Szálasi's Arrow Cross government I never finished the school year.

War

In the spring of 1944 my father obtained false documents for me in the name of Ilona Papp. With the help of Maria Babar, a devout Catholic, who had previously worked for our family but was then a secretary in the Ministry of War. I was hidden by the Ursuline nuns in their convent in Transdanubia (Dunántúl). By the fall, convents and monasteries had become targets of the SS and the Arrow Cross, who searched for Jews hidden by nuns and priests, so Maria brought me to her studio apartment in Buda, where my maternal grandmother and one of my mother's sisters had fled after being evicted by the woman who had promised to hide them. The four of us lived in the tiny apartment next door to the SS office, who luckily didn't suspect the true identity of their neighbors. Toward the end of December, the Siege of Budapest began, and we were obliged to spend the winter in the basement of the house, miraculously surviving although the house above us was completely destroyed by cannons, gunfire, and bombs. We were liberated in February 1945 by the Soviet army. In the meantime, my parents had been deported to Bergen-Belsen. They survived and returned from Switzerland in the spring of 1945.

Postwar

We tried to resume our normal lives in our renovated apartment. In 1947, I entered grade five in the *Mária Terézia gimnázium* (secondary school) in Budapest. By 1948, it was obvious that my father, a businessman, had no future under the Communist government. My mother even spent a few days at the notorious AVO (Hungarian KGB) headquarters on *Andrássy út*. We managed to flee to Austria in the fall of 1948, finally boarding, in Bremen, the *SS Scythia* for Canada, where my mother's sister was our sponsor. I was twelve years old when we settled in Montreal, and I was enrolled in the neighborhood Iona Avenue School at the end of sixth grade without any knowledge of English or French. By the end of grade seven, I had mastered enough of the language to qualify for a high school scholarship. Even though my parents spoke both languages, they found it very difficult to acculturate. I graduated from West Hill High School in 1954, earned a teacher's certificate at Macdonald College and a BA at Sir George Williams College (now Concordia) and taught elementary school.

Later life to the present

In 1957, I married Tevia Abrams, with whom I share many interests. We interspersed study (graduate work at Michigan State University), work, and travel (at first to Europe and later twice to India). Tevia worked for the UN in New York and India, and I taught French and English as a second language at the United Nations International School till we both retired in New York. We have two sons (in Chicago and Montreal) and one grandson, with whom we love to spend time in our second home in Montreal.

Schutzpass *Photo*
Budapest 1944

Marika Barnett

THE END

The terrible news arrived around Christmas, 1944. At first we thought that it was just one of the dozens of rumors circulating the city. Soon enough we realized that this rumor was real. The fascist Arrow Cross Party had decided to take matters into their own hands. From the middle of December, working dilligently through the Christmas holidays, they systematically collected the Jews from the buildings with Yellow Stars, led them by the thousands to the banks of the Danube, and shot them into the icy waters.

The raids were getting closer and closer to our house. We learned to estimate quite accurately the rate of their advance. The Russian troops were also advancing and we could hear the sound of their artillery on the outkirts of Budapest. We knew that the "brothers"(as they called themselves) of the Arrow Cross would probably reach us in Szent István-Park before the Soviet Army could liberate us.

My father still went to his office in Hegedüs Sándor-utca every day. He had inherited a successful wholesale bicycle company from my grandfather. Though the Germans had completely emptied his warehouses, he still found "important things" to do in the empty office. Since he was a man who always marched to the sound of his own drummer, my family had long ago stopped questioning him.

A few days before the New Year, the guard at the gate of our Yellow Star house, told us to get ready immediately. They were coming for us. They randomly selected families to be transported to the concentration camps. Shaking, we packed a few essentials into bags and suitcases and, to the accompaniment of tears from friends and neighbors, proceeded to the gate, where we were ordered at gunpoint to follow our guides. We must have been a sad sight indeed! We felt eyes watching us from behind the windows of the surrounding buildings. We had seen this happen to others many times. This time it was us!

I, a ten-year-old, held onto my parents' hands, and my two aunts followed us. An Army Corporal and an Arrow Cross Brother pointed their guns at us while roughly prodding us along. We were practically running since it was very close to the general curfew hour of 5 PM, and the Arrow Cross Party patrols were instructed to shoot anyone on the street after that hour. As we crossed the Oktogon, we saw the Pók Department Store burning. A bomb had hit it that afternoon. It was two minutes after 5 o'clock that we arrived in front of the building of Teréz Boulevard #6. This was the building that, from the side street, housed my father's offices. I didn't understand why we stopped there.

Our escorts banged on the barricaded gates while we stood on the wide, empty boulevard, in clear sight of marauding patrols. Though someone soon answered the desperate knockings and, after a brief checking, allowed us in, to us it seemed like an eternity. By that time I was prepared for anything. The fact that SS soldiers were waiting behind the gates didn't surprise me much. The surprise was that they didn't show any hostility. Within minutes we were across the inner courtyard of the building, entering the backrooms of my father's offices. Our two escorts were following us at every step and their presence still filled me with dread. It seemed inexplicable that my father didn't even try to get rid of them. Instead, without removing his coat he pulled out a bottle of brandy from a shelf, filled three small glasses and we heard with bewilderment the three men toast: "L'Chaim!"

We soon learned that our guides were two brave young Jewish volunteers. From their and my father's story we learned that, along with another thousand Jews, we were now under the protection of the German SS. More than fifty years later, I found out that SS Major Kurt Becher charged twenty thousand dollars for each family who moved into the twin buildings of Teréz Boulevard 6 and 8. My father never mentioned what it cost him to save his family's life.

Armed German soldiers and members of the SS guarded us against the Arrow Cross patrols, often using violence against them. They also provided uniforms and guns for such escort that brought us there. Everyone in the house got three meals a day. We were among the fortunate ones who didn't need food from the community kitchen. We had food that lasted well into the spring of 1945. To our amazement, we found out how my father had spent his time "at the office" since the German occupation. The storage room was furnished with 5 beds, a table, chairs and a giant stove. Shelves and cabinets were stocked with dried and canned foods, flour, lard, and so on. My father, who we thought, couldn't help himself to a glass of water, knew exactly what five people needed for survival. When he started to collect the supplies from Gentile friends and grateful employees, he only had a vague feeling that we might need a place to hide. It was through a miraculous coincidence that his offices happened to be located in one of the two buildings selected by the SS for the protection of a small percentage of the Budapest Jews.

We settled down in the backroom of the office. The adults played cards or chatted during the day, but I had nothing to do. In the rush, we hadn't thought of bringing books from home. I was absolutely miserable. My father came to the rescue again. Since his offices represented the Dunlop Company of England for many years, he had received from them a large album published after the coronation of King George the VI. That was the only book on the premises and I became very well versed in all the important details concerning the British Royal Family.

The Soviet army was getting close, and a shell hit our building, scattering bricks all over the courtyard. It was decided that we should move down into the basement's coal-cubicle that belonged to my father's office. It was a tiny space, where we could only sit in an upright position. We couldn't cook, of course, so we only ate canned tuna and sardines. Luckily, we also had several large boxes of cookies. Soon, we even had to share that small space with two other families who had no place of their own in the basement. It was dark. During the day some light filtered through the tiny basement windows, with the glass all broken from the constant bombings. We learned to make small lamps out of empty tuna cans that we filled with oil. We covered a cork with a small piece of metal that we cut out from the top of the can, threaded a string in the middle and floated the cork on the oil. The lamp gave out a lot of smoke and very little light. I discovered that there was a greater hunger than that for food, a greater thirst than for water. I hungered for light. This hunger consumed all my thoughts. Several coal-bins down the corridor, one lucky family had a miner's lamp. It gave out a wonderful, bright light. I knelt near the wall of our cell, buried my face between the dividing wooden slats, and stared at that light all day long. I wasn't peeping. I just wanted to feed my starving eyes with light.

Our German guards deserted us one by one. Hitler had ordered the SS to leave the defense of Budapest to the Wehrmacht and leave before the Soviet troops reached the city. SS Major Kurt Becher and his men were long gone. Wehrmacht Lieutenant Ludwig shot himself in the foot and was carried away by the Red Cross. Only one, SS Sergeant Ganzner, stayed with us. He didn't follow orders. Sergeant Ganzner understood that if he left, the Hungarian Fascists, who knew only too well who was hiding behind the closed gates of Teréz Boulevard 6 and 8, would empty the buildings immediately. Ganzner, an Austrian member of the SS, stayed to protect us.

By January 17th we knew that the Russians were just around the corner. We suspected that they knew about the Germans in our building and might use great force to break through. The Jewish men were asked to barricade the basement windows with the bricks from the courtyard. The men—cold, weak, hungry, and tired—ignored our request and left the windows as they were.

Sergeant Ganzner had been whisked away in civilian clothes, through the tunnels that connected the neighboring basements, and was hidden in the attic of a house nearby. Several weeks later, when it was safe, grateful Jews smuggled him to Czechoslovakia. From there Ganzner tried to go back to his native country, Austria, but on the way he was captured and shot by the Soviet army.

On the evening of January 17th, as the Soviet troops were approaching, we sent a committee to the Gentile tenants of our building. The air raid shelter had been exclusively theirs. It was clearly understood that only Gentiles were allowed into the shelter. Fearing a violent attack that night, our committee begged them to allow the Jewish children to take refuge in the shelter for that one night. The response was prompt: "No Jews in our shelter!"

No one slept that night. Near dawn, a horrendous explosion shook our building. Smoke spread quickly through the basement corridors. We knew we were going to die, and we were ready for it. My mother put my head into her lap, and we all anticipated to be suffocated. Time went by, and I was certain that I was dead. I had to be. What will this other world look like? I lifted my head, and in the faint light of dawn, that seeped through the broken basement windows, I saw with great disappointment that everything was still the same, and I was not in heaven. We were all still there. Through the basement windows that our men had refused to barricade, fresh air had come in. We soon found out what the large explosion had been. The Soviets - suspecting that Germans were hiding behind the gates – had thrown in a powerful bomb. The explosion tore through the five story building. Cement, brick, stone and metal came down on top of the air raid shelter. There were no survivors in there. We all stood there in silence, then quietly walked away.

January 18th, we were free. We had survived World War II. Soon we returned to the Yellow Star house in Szent István-park. Our beautiful apartment at Széchenyi-rakpart 12/b was burned and looted by Russian soldiers along with all the others. Only the American Embassy had money to rebuild it later and their employees lived there for over 40 years.

As the concentration camps got liberated one by one, we waited for our relatives to return. When all hope was gone, we started to mourn. We never stopped.

Out of my large, healthy family only one cousin returned from Auschwitz to her village in Northeast Hungary, by then occupied by the Soviet Union. Soon she was arrested, falsely charged and sentenced by the communists to 25 years of hard labor in Siberia.

Budapest 1953

Stow, Massachusetts 2005

Name: Marika Barnett (née Marika Schweitzer)

Born: Budapest 1934

Paternal Grandparents	**Maternal Granparents**
Grandfather	**Grandfather**
József Schweitzer	Mayer Fendrich
B: Losonc,1861	**B:** Mezőkaszony (Bereg m), 18??
D: Budapest, 1926	**D:** Mezőkaszony, 1938
Grandmother	**Grandmother**
Katalin (née Gelb)	Fáni (née Riedermayer)
B: Gyöngyös, 1864	**B:** Mezőkaszony (Bereg m.), 18??
D: Budapest 1955	**D:** Mezőkaszony, 1944
Father:	**Mother**
Kornél Schweitzer	Lenke (née Fendrich)
B: Jászárokszállás, 1887	**B:** Mezőkaszony (Bereg m.), 1895
D: Budapest, 1963	**D:** Budapest, 1983

Prewar

I lived in Budapest, Széchenyi-Rakpart 12/b. Father owned Atlas Gépkereskedelmi Részvénytársaság (bicycle wholesale company), English/Hungarian Kindergarden, then Szemere Street Elementary School. Continued 4th grade as a private student because of increasing anti-Semitism in school.

War

Moved to Yellow Star House in *Szent István Park*. First, I was hiding as a Gentile girl for a month in the industrial suburbs of the city, then I returned to my parents. From October 12 to December 12, I was hiding in a convent with nuns. They baptized me on December 11th. On the very next day, worried about my safety in the convent, my Father came for me and took me "home". (I wish he had come just 24 hours earlier!) At the end of December, we moved into the backroom of my Father's business. In that building, - in *Teréz Boulvard* 6 - the German SS saved 1,000 Jews, $20K per family. That is where we stayed until liberation.

Postwar

From my large and healthy family, only one cousin returned from Auschwitz. My two widowed aunts stayed with us for the rest of their lives. The land my mother's family owned belonged by now to the Soviet Union. My father's business was nationalized. We had suddenly become very poor! I finished high school and college before I escaped in 1956.

Later life to Present

Living in the USA since early 1957. Two sons: Alexander works in the financial world; Erik is Asst. US Attorney in Washington, DC. For the moment, two grandchildren: Sam and Julia. For 25 years I worked as a Software Engineer. In retirement, I became a published photographer and write plays.

Budapest, aged 2

Susan Bendor, Ph.D

The Ice Cream Man

In my story, I want to highlight what a profound character-forming difference one small act of kindness by a caring individual can make in the life of a young child who is bewildered and saddened by the discrimination she faces and the ordinary privileges of childhood she has lost by virtue of being a Jew, a reason she is not old enough to fully understand.

I was six years old in Budapest when our apartment building was designated as a "Jewish House" with a large yellow star placed above its gate. We were therefore able to remain in our apartment for a few months, now crowded with several friends and former employees of my father, who joined us to avoid having to move into the ghetto.

The Jewish Laws imposed by the Arrow Cross imposed more and more restrictions on Jews. For example, I was not allowed to go to school, appear at public events like a dance recital, and Jews were only allowed to shop one hour a day, from 10-11 A.M. when long lines stretched for blocks at bakeries and all other stores.

One afternoon, my mother, a big believer in fresh air, insisted on taking me for a walk, with both of us wearing our respective yellow stars stitched tightly to our clothes.

I was delighted to get out of our crowded flat and asked my mother to walk to the Italian ice cream store two blocks away, my favorite place in the world before the Holocaust changed everything. Upon our arrival there, I asked to go in, and my mother patiently explained to me that I could not buy ice cream now because we were Jews, and she had no money with her since we could not go into any stores in the afternoon.

I began to howl with disappointment and anger, crying being one of the few tools children have to communicate their emotions. In those years, attracting the attention of the Arrow Cross was a recipe for disaster. My mother quickly whisked me into the nearest courtyard. She begged me to stop crying, removed my yellow star, and gave me the penny she found in her pocket, allowing me to cross the street by myself to go into the ice cream store. The ice-cream man, who had clearly witnessed the entire scene through the window, greeted me warmly and gave me three scoops of ice cream for my penny.

I went from the depths of childish despair to the heights of victorious delight, knowing that a penny did not buy you three scoops even if you were not a Jew. The ice cream man's friendly kindness alleviated my sense of danger and fear of strangers carefully inculcated into me by my parents since the War began. These fleeting moments of security and delight were short- lived. As I was walking back home, happily licking my ice cream, we encountered Mrs. H., our superintendent's wife, a well-known Fascist who hated Jews. My mother turned pale and shivered next to me. If Mrs. H. noticed the missing yellow star from my skinny body, that could mean death for us since the rule was that yellow stars had to be worn at all times and had to be stitched so tightly that no finger could fit between stitches. A missing or loosely sewn star was grounds for being shot into the Danube river almost immediately. I suddenly understood my mother's terror and when Mrs. H., the super's wife, asked me to come closer to give her a hug, I answered in my sweetest voice, "Oh, Ms. H., I am so messy now, I'd rather wait until we all get home so I can come down to your apartment and give you the biggest clean kiss you ever had."

My coping skills were already developed at a young age, and my capacity to sense and respond to danger was mature beyond my years.

Fortunately, Mrs. H. did not turn us in to the authorities for my missing star, although she extorted money from my mother for her silence, and we lived in terror of her for the rest of our days in the building until we had to go into hiding.

Nevertheless, the memory of the generous, caring ice cream man not only sustained my hope and faith in the presence of good people during the subsequent months of hiding and persecution; his inspiring behavior has been incorporated into my character. As a professional social worker I see my primary role as being there for people when they are coping with challenges and problems often beyond their control, when they most need a caring ally and advocate for justice.

I am certain that the ice cream man, should he still be alive, probably would not remember the incident I described, but the three scoops of forbidden ice cream have left an indelible impact on my life and professional career.

The Cellar

The nine months from about May 1944 to Liberation, we spent in a cellar in the Nagymezö utca in Budapest. There was a German uniform factory in the building, where my aunt had been ordered to work. She begged the officer in charge to hide me and my brother, who was juvenile diabetic, in the cellar. At first he said no because children made noise, but then he allowed not only us but also two other Jewish families to hide there, one of whom had a beautiful teenage daughter called Bébi (Baby). The other Jewish couple was deaf mute.

We never knew the last names of the German officer or his aide. We just knew them as Officer Wuchte and his aide as, Martin. This was as much for their safety as ours.

We survived on food brought to us by a former employee of my father's, Nándi Bácsi* and by the Gentile wife of our attorney. When necessary, we raided the barrels of fermenting sauerkraut that were in the cellar. One day, Nándi Bácsi brought us horsemeat and we feared that it had to be the flesh of one of the horses that we knew from the neighborhood. My brother and I speculated long and hard on which one it could be and whether we could eat the meat but in the end hunger won out over guilt. Ever since, I have been afraid of horses and can't bear to even look at sauerkraut.

The superintendent of the building sometimes allowed each family in turn to spend a night upstairs in his apartment, in order to get away from the stench of the cellar and to get some rest and fresh air. Even though he was getting paid for this, he was taking a big risk. I was unwell the night it was our turn to go upstairs, and my mother thought it better not to move me, so we gave up our turn in favor of the deaf mute man and the other family. That night, there was a bombing raid and our building was hit. The superintendent's apartment was destroyed, and beautiful Bébi suffered terrible disfigurement, while the deaf mute man lost his sight. That night, I heard my father wailing, "There is no G-d! There is no G-d!"

Martin was able to pass Bébi off as his girlfriend to get her to a hospital to be treated for severe burns.

There were two conditions in the cellar that caused the most contention among its occupants. The first one was over the single small candle that was allowed to burn to give us a source of light. Everybody wanted to be next to it, but it was my mother who had priority. She needed the light to give my brother his insulin shots. She had been hoarding insulin since the beginning of the war, and she carried it around with her in a red leather bag that hung on her wrist and never left her. She also took this opportunity to surreptitiously take out a little tube of face cream and massage some into her face. This daily little vanity was a reassurance to us children. If Mother still bothered to keep herself beautiful, she could not be expecting us to be killed!

The other bone of contention was the bucket that served as our toilet and which had to be emptied every night. It was a chore that had fallen to the men, and there was always an argument as to whose turn it was to do that distasteful and dangerous chore. The waste had to be taken upstairs, into the street, and poured into the sewer. We always held our breath until the unhappy candidate returned.

We were liberated by the Soviets in January. The adults went looking for Wuchte and Martin to vouch for them in front of the conquering Soviet authorities, but we didn't know their last names. They were never found, and the Soviets told us that "They did not take prisoners"

We were never able to thank them, nor their families, or even send their names to Yad Vashem.

---

*Bácsi: "Uncle" A address that children use toward older men. The feminine equivalent is "néni"

New York, Stony Brook 1975

New York 2007

Name: Susan Bendor (née Blum Zuzsanna (Zsuzsi) Julianna)

Born: Budapest, 1937

Paternal Grandparents	**Maternal Grandparents**
Grandfather	**Grandfather**
Gershon Blum	Julius Weisz
B: Unknown	**B:** Pozsony, 1864
D: Budapest	**D:** Györ, 1923
(Sometime during the war)	
Grandmother	**Grandmother**
Malka (née?)	Lenke (née Freund)
B: Unknown	**B:** Pozsony , 1884
D: Auschwitz 1944	**D:** Budapest 1951
Father:	**Mother**:
David Blum	Elizabeth (née Weisz)
B: Budapest 1905	**B:** Galanta, Csechoslovakia, 1911
D: Montreal 1989	**D:** Montreal 1997

Prewar

My life before the war was a very middle class existence in Budapest. My father had a successful textile business. I took ballet lessons and spent summers in our villa, named after me, in *Balatonszéplak*. My brother's juvenile diabetes was the major stress factor in our lives. Due to my age and the war, I did not start school until after we were liberated on January 18, 1945

War

See my story, "The Cellar", above.

Postwar

We lived in Vienna for two years and in Zurich for 6 months while waiting for conditions in the newly founded State of Israel to become stable enough for us to immigrate there, and be assured of an uninterrupted supply of insulin for my only brother. In 1951, when the Korean War broke out, my father feared that it was the start of World War III and we quickly emigrated to Montreal, Canada where we needed to learn both English and French. I began to study day and night to do well in school and make up for all the scorn I experienced earlier as a Jewish child having to wear a yellow star. I began to win awards and went on to acquire several degrees, including a doctorate in social work. I met my husband in Montreal and immigrated with him to the U.S. in 1960. I traveled a lot and spent a year studying at Heidelberg University. We now have two terrific daughters and granddaughters and I have held a variety of clinical, administrative and academic jobs as a professional social worker. I am still teaching as an Associate Professor at the *Wurzweiler* School of Social Work, Yeshiva University. The fight for social justice and the prevention of human suffering, wherever it takes place, have been the driving forces in my life during the last forty years

Judit and her brother at her cousin Magda's wedding.
Both bride and groom perished.

Judith Bihaly

TRUTH AND IMMORTALITY

The office where my father attended to his patients contained a dentist's chair, a tall, stainless steel wash cabinet with sink and faucet—whose tank had to be manually filled with water and whose drain barrel had to be manually emptied, since it was not connected to any plumbing—and a dentist's drill that he operated by pumping on a foot-pedal. He liked the control he had over the gentle speed of the drill, which he could stop at will when a patient raised a finger to indicate pain. I know this because in those days patients didn't guard their privacy and many enjoyed letting a cute, well-behaved, and relaxing six- or seven-year-old little girl watch.

Next to the entrance to this room stood a "*vitrin*," a glass cabinet whose glass shelves displayed plaster of paris molds of teeth, dentures, wax molds of dentures, gold crowns, and a large assortment of Bakelite samples in different colors—the stuff that dentures, bridges, and crowns were made of. You may surmise that at the end of the thirties, in Budapest, many dentists were their own dental technicians, "masters" in the waning days of the old guild system.

My father's second territory was his work area next to the window in our large kitchen, which looked out on the "*gang*," or courtyard terrace, of our second-floor apartment in Budapest and which flooded the space with light even on cloudy days. The entire surface of his work table was covered with pink sheets of wax, bits of wax, plaster of paris teeth, little hammers used to fashion gold crowns, pliers, wires, Bunsen burners, a kiln, and there were drops of melted wax everywhere. Bridges and dentures were in various stages of completion. His dentist's drill in this room was powered by electricity that once gave me a shock, teaching me never to touch it again. When my father was in this space, and I was home, the space also contained me—talking incessantly, happily, and easily about anything that came into my mind. I was constantly touching and handling things as I yakked away, without feeling any need to censor myself and without worry whether my father listened or understood, secure in knowing that he loved having me around even though he was not an affectionately demonstrative man.

By the way, the working part of the kitchen was not heavily used, because my mother, too, had her own larger business in the part of our apartment overlooking the street. She was a master dressmaker with almost a dozen apprentices and journeyman assistants. She catered to actresses and wives or concubines of ministers and military officers of high rank. She affectionately called them her favorite "*kurvák*" (whores). You can surmise by now that we owned a very large apartment at Jokai utca, 40, on the second floor. I can still recite our phone number: "*száz huszon eggy, nulla harminc négy*" (121-034). We lived there, too, and food was sometimes delivered from *Ilkovics* restaurant (mostly for my father), sometimes cooked by one of my mother's apprentices, and sometimes cooked by my mother when she felt like it or when company was coming. She was a great cook. There were seldom any family meals in this busy household as my twin brother, András, and I were mostly sent to live with families outside Budapest and brought home when school was closed for the summer. But that's another story.

The story I want to tell is one that sustains my father in my heart to this day. I might have been seven years old, and my father was showing me what "elasticity" really meant. He held a rubber ball up high and let it drop, catching it as it bounced. Then he took a shiny white ball of Bakelite out of his *vitrin* and let it drop, hardly lowering his hand to catch it, since unlike the rubber ball, the Bakelite ball bounced almost back into his hand. Years later, in my physics classes, I understood elasticity and related concepts with ease. I always knew, whenever he answered a question or explained something, that he did it with love and respect (no laughter or "Oh, how cute!") and I felt safe. On this day, the question I asked him concerned the frequent references in school and in the school's chapel to the Virgin Mary. I asked my father "What is a virgin?"

I could tell I touched a nerve, because my father sucked in a deep breath and then paused to think. He said that I was probably too young to be told everything about virginity, but that it had to do with love between a man and a woman. He said that a virgin was a woman who had never been loved by a man, and then he promised to tell me more if I asked him when I was older. That I still didn't really know what a virgin was didn't matter, because in the moment when he finished I learned my most important lesson about my father. I learned he would never lie to me, no matter what.

I was the last person in my family to see my father, at the age of nine in the summer of 1944, when he was summoned to report for forced labor outside Budapest. He came to my hiding place to tell me he would not be visiting for a while. In November 2005, on a visit to the Museum of Hungarian Speaking Jewry in C'fat (Safed), Israel, I learned for the first time when and how he had died.

Whenever I wonder how we have remained human after all we lost as children—after we lost everything, how we have held on to those we lost—the answer for me is the memory of my father's definition of "virgin." His respect for his young daughter, his unconditionally loving truth, has been the rock that keeps him alive in me. As long as I am still alive, so is he.

Atlantic City, NJ 1951

New Jersey 2007

Name: Judith Bihaly (née Judit Bihály)

Born: 1934, Budapest

Paternal Grandparents
Grandfather
Ignác Bihály
B: Unknown,

D: Unknown

Grandmother
Ida (née Patek)
B & D: Unknown

Maternal Grandparents
Grandfather
Jakab Nettel, Jewish Hungarian Huszár
abandoned wife and three children in
Baja, Hungary
B & D: Unknown

Grandmother
Regina (née Baumgarten)
B: Vienna, Austria, date unknown
D: Baja, Hungary, 1936

Father
Károly Bihály
B: 1893, Gyoma
D: 1944, Kőszeg (forced labor)
(children's 10th birthday)

Mother:
Jozefa (née Nettel)
B. 1906, Miklusevci, Yugoslavia.
D: 1996, New Jersey

Brother: Bihály András. B: December 16, 1934, Budapest (Judit's twin). **D:** September 11, 1968, New York City. Suicide

Prewar

My parents married January 29, 1934, six months after my father's first wife died in childbirth. His infant son died soon after his second wedding; my twin brother András and I were born in December later that year. At age two, we were placed in Tante Elsa's German *"ovoda,"* sometimes just during the day and sometimes overnight, freeing our parents to pursue their businesses: father, *"fogteknikus mester"* (Master Dental Technician), and mother, *"szabó mester."* (Master Tailor). Being far younger than any of the children at Tante Elsa's, we succumbed to a succession of life-threatening infections and illnesses till we were sent to live in Rákospalota (a Budapest suburb) with a succession of strange families, resulting in emotional traumas but improved physical health. Mother visited us on Sundays with her boyfriend, and father visited on Wednesdays. Our schooling during the first two elementary grades was in Rákospalota public schools (same as Catholic parochial schools in the United States). In 1939, we were baptized. We didn't know we were Jewish.

War

1943-1945: In late 1943 we returned home to Jókai u. 40. We attended public school. Father was charged with taking us to Catholic Mass on Sundays. I was fervently Catholic. A few months after the March 1944 German occupation, András was hidden in a suburban *"javító intézet,"* (Reform School) and I was hidden by the Catholic priest Klinda Pál (listed among the Just at Yad Vashem) in the Catholic girls' finishing school that he directed on Budakeszi út in Buda. Mother was deported to Auschwitz, which she survived. Father visited me twice, the second time saying good-bye and explaining that he was called up to work at the *téglagyár* and would not be able to visit for a while (never seen again). Searching for my father, I imagined him lost but still alive into my forties. I finally learned how he died in 2005. Sometime in the fall of 1944, I was abandoned (possibly because mother's trusted friend had stolen my ration cards and because of other circumstances that had developed at Father Klinda's hiding place) and taken to another estate on Budakeszi út from where children were regularly taken, ten at a time, to be shot into the Duna. Soviet liberation came on Christmas, 1944. Mother was liberated at Terezin and walked home; she eventually found András and me in two different *"vidéki"* (Country) places where we had been placed after the war by the *Nemzeti Segély,* (National Aid Society)

Postwar

1945–1947: Mother placed us in a *pluga* (group home) run by the Zionist group Dror Habonim, where we finally learned that we were Jewish. Our youth *alyah* group (plus our mother) left Hungary in December 1946. Mother came with us as our "nurse," using the Zionist Schlichim to cross the closed Hungarian border in order to emigrate to the United States. After a succession of DP camps and Zionist group homes through Austria, Germany, and Italy, she separated from our group and took my brother to live in a DP camp. I refused to go with her, and with my youth *alyah* group, I arrived in Israel in the fall of 1947. According to the Palyam records in the Palmach Museum in Tel Aviv (dedicated in November 2005), our boat was one of only two that succeeded in evading the British on the way to Israel.

1947–1950: I developed my sense of self during the period I lived with my youth group, called *aliyat hanoar tet,* in Europe and at Kibbutz Ashdot Yaakov, until mother succeeded in forcing me to join her and Andrew in a DP camp awaiting admission to the United States.

1950-1969: I learned English; attended night school and graduated high school; and earned a bachelor's of science in psychology from CCNY, all while working as a secretary in a law firm. I Married Miki Kohn (a survivor from Budapest) in October 1956. Our son Kenneth was born April 15, 1962. We lived in Montvale, New Jersey. I worked at the research facility at Rockland State Hospital from 1966 to 1969. I lost my brother to suicide in 1968.

Later life to the present

1969–2007: I earned my master's of education in mathematics and became a mathematics teacher in 1972.

I became surrogate mother in 1975 to Peter, age twelve, whose single mother (Miki's cousin) died.

I divorced Miki in March 1987, three days after Kenneth's wedding to Claudia and almost one year after Peter's wedding to Ellen. I moved from Montvale to Edgewater, New Jersey.

I began practicing yoga in 1986 and became a certified Kripalu yoga teacher in 1996. I retired from teaching math in 1998, but continued to teach yoga till 2004, stopping only after I contracted a muscle-wasting disease (inclusion body myositis). My newfound interest, folk dancing, has helped arrest progression of the disease (at least for now).

Kenneth and Claudia have lived in London, U.K. since 1999; they have four children, born between 1991 and 1998: Saul, Hannah, Yosef, and Ezra. Kenneth works for Bloomberg Business News.

Peter and Ellen live in Ardsley, New York. Their daughter Hedy was adopted in 1992, and Jacob was born in 1993. He is a guidance counselor, and she has a private practice working with autistic children.

With Mother, Paris 1941

Evi Blaikie

AIR RAID*

It was sometime in the spring of 1944, after the Germans had entered Hungary, that the Allied bombing of Budapest started and we became frequent visitors to the cellar under our apartment building.

The radio was always left on in order to be able to hear the air raid warnings signaling incoming enemy planes. The music would be interrupted and we'd hear the mysterious warning, *"Achtung, achtung! Lichtspiel Krokodil … Légiriado."* After that, names of towns were listed, one after the other, to let us know where the planes had been spotted approaching the capital, and we'd know when it was time to run down to the cellar.

We lived on the fifth floor of an apartment building in the fifth district called Lipot Város, a largely well-to-do Jewish neighborhood populated by many who had migrated from the ghetto. My family's business was still situated there, but the ghetto was no longer considered elegant enough to live in by my upwardly mobile family. The building had been designated as a "Jewish House" , which meant that a large Star of David was painted on the front door, and Jews were to be moved in, one family to every room. Christian families could stay in their apartments if they wanted to. We were expecting three more families to move in with us very shortly.

Our apartment had a balcony, which was attached to the balcony of the apartment next door, but separated by a floor-to-ceiling opaque glass wall, so that if we wished to talk to our neighbors face to face, we had to lean out toward the street, past the divider. Naturally, we children were never allowed to lean over the balcony railings. Wooden boxes with plants in them had been placed along the floor of the balcony to block the space between it and the bottom of the railing to prevent us from slipping through and falling to the street below.

It was a particularly warm and sunny spring day. Peter, my cousin who was ten years old, and I, at five years old, were allowed to go out and play on the balcony. The heavy wooden blinds, called *rollo*, were lowered so the sun's ray would not damage the upholstery and the rugs inside. The wide sliding doors however were left open, and as usual, the radio was on.

Peter and I were engrossed in our play when suddenly we heard the interruption. *"Achtung, Achtung, Lichtspiel, Krokodil …"* We immediately turned to go back inside, but the heavy wooden blinds barred our way. We shouted to the adults, "There's an air raid warning. Let us in!" We heard my aunt Klari coming, and she took hold of the rope that was attached to the pulley which controlled the blinds. The rope was stuck. She couldn't budge it. She called for help, and Aunt

43

Kati and my mother came running. There were no men in the household anymore. They had been called up for forced labor duty, *munkaszolgálat*.

The three sisters yanked on the rope together and managed to raise it a few inches. "Come on, kids, slide through," they urged. As I wiggled under the blinds, flat on my stomach, half in, half out over the sill, the rope broke and several inches of heavy wooden slats came crashing down on my legs. I started to howl, and the women screamed. Finally my aunts got down to the floor and managed to prop up the slats just enough that my mother was able to pull me through. A quick examination proved that my legs were still attached to the rest of me, not even broken, just bruised. I, however, was crying uncontrollably, not just because it hurt but also because Peter was still outside on the balcony and the voice on the radio was starting to call out the towns the bombers were flying over. They were headed toward Budapest.

Peter was panicking. He was terrified of bombs. "Let me in, let me in! Do something!" he screamed. My mother ran next door, banged on the door and was immediately let in. "The balcony," she panted, "Peter is stuck there! There's an air raid warning." She ran through the apartment to the balcony, leaned out toward the street and called to Peter on the other side. "Come on, darling, you'll have to climb over. I'll hold your hand."

My two aunts and I had followed her. I was crying and limping—and totally ignored. My aunt Klari, Peter's mother, was getting hysterical. "No, he can't do that! He'll fall. You can't let him do that!"

"He will NOT fall" said my mother, "He's as agile as a monkey. Do you want him to stay out there alone during an air raid?"

Peter was scared. It was five flights up. The radio was droning on: "*Sopron … Györ … Pápa … Tata … Dorog …*" The planes were getting closer. He put his legs over the railing, out over the street, and started inching over to the balcony next door. He needed both hands to hang on; the sisters could only watch. As one hand grabbed the balcony railing on the other side of the divider, his foot slipped, and we heard a scream. Aunt Klari fainted, but my mother had already grabbed Peter's wrist, and he regained his footing. As he was climbing back onto the neighbor's balcony, Aunt Kati grabbed his other hand, and both women pulled him in so hard they all fell backward in a pile, knocking the rest of us down. As we scrambled to our feet, we could already hear the engines of the planes. My mother bent over her sister Klari, gave her two sharps slaps on the face, and said impatiently, "Get up! This is not the time to faint. Peter's fine. Let's go!" She helped her sister to her feet, and we all rushed down to the cellar, where we stayed, huddled together, listening to the sound of explosions until the "all clear" sounded.

The following day, Aunt Kati came home with the identity papers she had acquired from a Christian family, and we got ready to go into hiding for the remainder of the war

---

* This story appeared in an abbreviated version in the book **Magda's Daughter,** *published by the Feminist Press at CUNY, 2003*

Between Feast and Famine

In the spring of 1944, with the identities that we had "borrowed" from Christian friends, we traveled west to a little village called *Lovászpatona,* in *Transdanubia,* about halfway between the industrial towns of Györ and Pápa. Our nanny-cum-maid of many years, Margit, was of the village and helped us obtain accommodations in a farmhouse whose owners she knew. We were introduced as a Christian family fleeing from the bombs falling on Budapest: mother, son, niece, and "governess." Father was supposed to be in the army fighting "on the right side." According to our identity papers, I was now my mother's niece, and my cousin Peter was her son.

We rented the front room of the farmhouse, the one with the windows facing the unpaved road that ran past the farm. It opened into a central multipurpose kitchen/living room that housed the huge floor-to-ceiling, tiled stove, the only source of warmth in the house during winter. Facing our room, across the central area, was the only other room, and it abutted the stables. In that room slept the entire peasant family: mother, father, four sons, and the grandfather

We eased nervously into our life in hiding, careful never to use our real names, only the ones in our acquired identity papers. Despite several close calls, our situation was fortunate compared to hundreds of thousands of other Jews. Our hosts were not malicious people, as opposed to several neighbors whose daily conversations over the fence always included the term "stinking Jews."

Though food was not abundant, we did not starve. A farm always yields some food, though toward the end of the war the Germans and the *Nyilas* were requisitioning most of the food supply for themselves, leaving us with potatoes, onions, and *szalonna* (smoked lard studded with garlic and coated with paprika). There was a cow in the barn, and I learned to milk it and squirt the milk directly into my mouth.

Peter and I had heard that people ate pigeons as a delicacy and that they tasted good. We decided to set some traps, but we had absolutely no idea how to go about it. We tried to copy a rat trap, but instead of the heavy spring that decapitated the rat, which we didn't have anyway, we used a thin wire attached to a piece of string that we then looped so when the pigeon ate the corn we left as bait, the string would coil around its legs and catch it. The project kept us busy, and every day we looked to see if we had snared a pigeon. It was always in vain.

One day a rumor swept the village that more German troops were coming through and they were going to be quartered in the farms overnight. My mother thought it was a good time for us to get out of town for a while, notwithstanding our newly acquired papers. Dressed in peasant clothes and carrying little bundles of whatever food was available, we left at dawn. We kept away from the main roads and just walked with no particular destination in mind.

We walked mostly through woods, resting now and then in some clearings, sleeping in an abandoned barn, and hoping the German troops would soon leave the village so we could go back to our hiding place.

At some point in our journey, we came upon a solitary little farmhouse with a neat garden in front and two huge bushes bearing large spiky fruit, which my mother identified immediately as artichokes. She was very surprised as artichokes were unknown in Hungary, but she had lived in France for many years and was familiar with them.

The farmer's wife came out of the house, and my mother asked her about the bushes. She didn't know what they were and said she was going to cut off "those ugly things and throw them in the garbage." My mother asked if she could have them and was told to take as many as she wanted. We loaded up on artichokes and slowly, wearily, headed home, hoping that the Germans had passed through.

We arrived back late at night and found out they had bypassed the village, and our short flight had been for naught. We were exhausted, but before we could go to bed, my mother had to make sure our blackout curtains didn't let any light through. A tiny sliver of light could be construed as a signal to an airplane and carried an immediate death sentence. She went outside to check and took longer than usual to come back in.

"I checked your traps," she said. "Pigeons would have tasted good with the artichokes."

The next morning, Peter went out with a determined look on his face and a mysterious bulge in his pocket. An hour later he was back with several fat, dead pigeons … and his deadly slingshot! My mother gutted and cleaned the pigeons, and that day we feasted on roast pigeons and artichokes.

It tasted wonderful to us.

With all that happened in hiding and in the intervening years, this episode remained a dormant memory until many years later when I saw, on the menu of a fancy New York restaurant, the following item: "Squab with pomegranate sauce, accompanied by roasted artichoke hearts."

Vienna 1960

New York 2005

Visit to Versailles 2007, with daughter Jennifer (L) and granddaughters,
Sophie (b.1992) and Maggie (Magda, b. 1990)

48

Name: Evi Blaikie, (née Evelyne Juliette Weisz)

Born: Paris, France, 1939

Paternal Grandparents	**Maternal Grandparents**
Grandfather	**Grandfather**
József Weisz	Miksa Pollák
B: Unknown	**B**: Pálfalva, Hungary, 1871
D: Nagyvárad (Oradea), 1906	**D**: Budapest, 1961
Grandmother	**Grandmother**
Lenke (née Fried)	Rozsa (née Freund)
B: Unknown	**B**: Simontornya, 1876
D: Auschwitz, 1944	**D**: Auschwitz, 1944
Father:	**Mother**
Hermann Weisz	Magda (née Pollák)
B: Nagyvárad, Transylvania, Hungary, 1900	**B:** Rákospalota, Hungary, 1912
(after 1918, Oradea, Romania)	**D:** London, England, 1964
D: Auschwitz, 1944	

Prewar

My mother and father had both emigrated to France, from Hungary and Transylvania, respectively, met, and married there. My father owned a small men's tailoring salon. I was born in Paris in January 1939.

War

When Paris was occupied, my father, a communist, went underground. In March 1941, my mother was caught in a *razzia* and deported to an ammunitions factory in Steiermark, Austria. I was taken to Hungary, which was still relatively safe at that time, to live with my mother's sisters. After two years, my mother escaped from the forced labor camp and managed to get to Hungary, where we were reunited just before the German invasion in 1944, at which point we went into hiding with forged identity papers. We hid on a farm in *Lovászpatona*, a village in *Transdanubia*. We were liberated by the Soviet army in the spring of 1945.

Postwar

My mother and I returned to Paris in January 1946. My father had disappeared, and it was only in 1954 that we found out that he had perished in Auschwitz. I was placed in the **Anna**

Szenes orphanage at *Verneuil-sur-Seine* (financed by the JOINT committee) while my mother tried to put our lives back together. In 1949, we emigrated to England. I lived at the Norwood Jewish Orphanage in south London and attended Saint-Martin-in-the-Fields High School for Girls. In 1957, I went to Vienna and attended university there. From Austria, I went to Caracas, Venezuela, and then came to New York in 1960.

Later life to the Present

In 1961, I was married to Donald Blaikie. We had three children: Jennifer (b. 1962), Nicholas (b. 1964), Peter (b. 1970). My mother died in London in 1964. I started a career in fashion and worked on Seventh Avenue for twenty-five years. I divorced in 1978. In 2003, I published my memoirs, *Magda's Daughter*. I now write and work part time in the environmental field and watch my grandchildren with awe: Maggie, Sophie, Henry, Joe, and Bailey.

Swedish Schutzpass 1944

52

Susan Charney

A War Story

I was around six years of age. We had once more moved to new quarters from the new city, Buda, back to the old city of Pest. Whenever my parents heard about a "comb out," we moved. I couldn't grasp the meaning of the words, only sensed the fear and anxiety. I was proud of my ability to remember our good Hungarian name, "Narancsi," and I understood that the stakes were high. Budapest was under siege. I had to be careful to keep this new name and to count the rosary beads whenever we went to the cellar. Upstairs, I could use my old name.

The bombardments were heavy, but we stopped going to the shelter. My sister and I were instructed to remain in the bathroom until the bombing ceased. I did as I was told even if it made no sense: how could it be safer in the bathroom than where the other people were?

One day, the sirens went off again. This time my parents took us and proceeded to exit through the building's gate. I think my father was carrying some belongings. I was walking beside him. At times he tried to carry me. The four of us were running through the city streets as the bombs were exploding around us. I saw a woman lying amongst the rubble, her head in an odd position and her breasts exposed. I asked, "Why is she lying like that?" I was told, "She is sleeping."

I knew she was not asleep, that I was being told nonsense. A vague image of this woman has remained in my mind. For some reason, I became preoccupied with her. I thought I should keep quiet, and someday I would solve the mystery of the woman and the madness of us running through the streets with everyone else in the cellars.

We got to another part of town by the time the bombardment had ended. In our new location we had a large apartment with a stained glass ceiling over the dining room and huge bay windows. After a while all the glass shattered, and we spent all our time in the cellar. There were many people in the shelter, and I had to resume using my new name. We settled into the coal bin away from the others. My mother wrapped up my face and my sister's face declaring that we had the mumps and that we had to remain in the makeshift quarantine of the coal bin. I didn't know why she said that we were sick. I tried to imagine what mumps was like. It had something to do with hiding our faces because we were brown-eyed with dark hair.

Many rumors circulated, like the one about the Russians who were going to come through the doors with flamethrowers. I tried to imagine what this would look like, the flames coming through the door. All of a sudden the Russians were in our cellar. A strange man put me in his lap. I was told to say nothing. A Hungarian soldier was stripping off his uniform in our coal bin and thrust his cap into my father's hand. The Russians started taking my father away.

Nothing made sense to me. The details were filled in by others afterward. I learned about the strange man who was a Nazi and had threatened to kill me. He escaped. My father was released. The soldier was taken away. I still remember the whispers about the building where we had previously stayed upstairs and the words, "They made them dance and then killed them all …" I wanted to know why they made them dance, but I never asked. I still don't have the answer.

The Visit to Kiskőrös

I recall a more quiet drama that happened after the war. My mother was accompanying us for the ride back to our family place in Kiskőrös. My mother, my sister and I, laughing and joking on the way as we got covered with dust riding in a convertible, keeping the top down for the experience. I had spent a number of sweet summers in the hubbub of my grandparents' home. My mother seemed happy, eager to return. My two uncles and a woman greeted us with joy. I saw my mother enter the doorway , when she suddenly turned, racked with sobs and, without a word, fled back into the car. I was shocked. Something was explained to me that I did not understand. I did not understand any of the remainder of my stay there. Everything seemed different. The garden was still there, but it was empty. There were no other children around. No one was at the large table for rolling out the pastry for *rétes* (strudel), no jars and chattering people for the canning of the rich fruits of summer. A woman who claimed to be my aunt kept giving me large slices of buttered bread. It turned into sawdust in my mouth, and I spat the bites out when no one was looking. The emptiness I felt inside and outside made no sense. A room I loved, with beautiful white furniture, was kept unused. I was given a different room.

My aunt Magdus remembers trying to feed me, worried about her thin, little niece. I remember, but I do not remind her, that to me she was not my aunt. I had known a different aunt, one who worried if I tried to hold her new baby. Yet she was married to the same uncle. I had dreamt of growing bigger, so they would let me hold the baby. No one could explain what happened. The summer heat hung in the air. It was a summer I thought would never end.

New York 1961

New York 2006

Name: Susan Charney (née (Zsuzsi Fried)

Born: Mezőkövesd, Hungary, 1938

Parternal Grandparents:	Maternal Grandparents:
Grandfather:	**Grandfather**
Yitzhak Fried	Jacob Klein
B: Place unknown, 1839	**B:** Place unknown, 1879
D: Mezőkövesd, 1915	**D:** Kiskőrös, 1933
Grandmother:	**Grandmother:**
Therese (née Goldberger)	Rachel (née Weiss)
B: Unknown	**B:** Huszt,1887
D: Israel, 1960s	**D:** Auschwitz, 1944
Father:	**Mother**
Alexander Samuel Fried	Hannah Hajnal (née Klein)
B: Mezőkövesd, 1902	**B:** Kiskőrös, 1907
D: Florida, United States, 1992	**D:** NewYork, 1981

Prewar

I was born in Mezőkövesd, Hungary, in 1938, five years after my sister, Judith. My parents came from venerable Hungarian towns. My mother is from Kiskőrös, the home of Hungary's poet laureate, Petöfi Sándor. His statue stands near a street where they once lived in their spacious family home. It is now a school. They were the owners of vineyards and orchards, the makers of wine. The building for their wine cellars remains intact, not far from the railroad tracks. My mother was one of five siblings—her mother and two brothers remained on the land. My Aryan-looking blonde, blue-eyed mother desperately tried to save her family. She succeeded in rescuing her youngest brother.

My paternal grandfather had founded a soda factory and a wholesale grocery store in the seat of Hungary's folk heritage, the town of Mezőkövesd, the home of the Hungarian peasant doll, Matyó baba. My father's mother was known for her domination; she retained absolute control of a prosperous business in Mezőkövesd, ultimately leading to my father's departure. With a wife and two children, he left his house and inheritance and went to try his luck in Budapest. There was no foretelling that this move in 1939 would one day prove to be instrumental in our survival. We escaped the fate of the extended family. They remained in the countryside, only to be more conveniently shipped away in cattle cars.

War

We arrived in Budapest when I was less than a year old. My parents were business partners in textile manufacturing. My father dreamed of running a single plant from A to Z, from wool to yarn to fabric. It was taken from him twice, first by Aryanization, and postwar, expropriated by the Communists.

We survived the *Shoah* in Budapest by evading collections, acquiring false papers, and switching identities from Jews to Christians and back again. We moved several times and maintained different locations. My father, who was easier to identify, was often confined to the apartment. In 1944, my father had sought plastic surgery to alter the Semitic shape of his nose. Still, he was recognized, identified by a "righteous" Hungarian citizen as a Jew, and promptly picked up and shipped away. He memorized the terrain and fled from a forced labor camp. He went by foot through the forest, avoiding people, and arrived back to our hiding place in Budapest so disheveled that I did not recognize him.

Postwar

Following the war, my parents reopened a textile plant. My father was arrested for being a businessman. I was questioned by the secret police. We fled Hungary in 1949 after my father's temporary release by the GRE, the Communist secret police. I have a copy of a photo he sent the GRE. He's wearing his custom-made suit and waving good-bye from under the statue of Maria Therese, clearly from the heart of Vienna.

We remained stranded in Vienna in 1949, awaiting entry permits to the West: Eastern European refugees were restricted by quotas. Vienna was a divided city, true to the images in *The Third Man*, full of refugees and wheeler-dealers; my parents enrolled me in the local public school. I shuddered at the sound of German, never quite grasping that the danger was over, dreading each day of school. All students attended daily religious Christian training. I had nowhere to go, petrified to reveal that I was Jewish. As if they did not know! Unable to follow any of the lessons, I spent my days reading books under the desk. We arrived in New York in 1949. My millionaire great uncle gave my father a job washing out refrigerators. My father contemplated suicide. As a Jew, my great uncle had been barred from attending medical school in Vienna. He had come to the States earlier and made his fortune. He never forgot the care packages from his beloved family in Kiskőrös. He sought to help us, yet he and his spouse were bewildered by the stories of horrific events and terrified by the potential horde of relatives and strange survivors knocking on his door, albeit we were few.

Life to the Present

True to the spirit of the American immigrant story, we managed. At the time, it was not fashionable to be a survivor. I concealed my past and pursued the American dream. I married an American. We had one son. I obtained a master's in social work and with advanced training became a psychoanalyst. My first social work job was with Selfhelp, working with aging émigrés. I have remained in the mental health field and have myself become an aging émigré.

Budapest 1941

Eva Cooper

Sadness, Despair, Fear, and Hope

Prior to March 1944, my family and I lived a privileged life. Many things were happening in Eastern Europe, but at first they did not touch me. However, the day after my tenth birthday, March 19, 1944, the Germans marched into and then occupied Budapest, and our world collapsed. On the eve of the invasion, all knew what was about to happen, and of course, my birthday party was over and everyone left in a hurry. I did not fully understand why.

Soon after my birthday, a new "Jewish Law" was passed. Each Jewish family would be allowed only one room in certain buildings designated as "Jewish Houses". Our building was so designated. We were now going to live in one room of our home. Three other families moved in. My aunt Ilus, her husband Károly, and their son Pali moved into my bedroom. My childhood friend Tommy and his parents moved into our dining room. Tommy's cousins were in the living room. My beautiful childhood home was not quite the same, under the new living circumstances. We lived this way from March until October of 1944.

The non-Jewish tenants of the building had the choice to either stay or to leave. A friend of mine from the building told me she could no longer play with me. I asked why. "Because you are Jewish," she said. I did not understand this, nor did she. She was just following her parents' directions. An act as simple as this allowed prejudice and hatred to be passed to the next generation. This was my own first realization that being Jewish made me different, and that in 1944, there was a high price to pay for being Jewish.

Unbeknownst to my mother, my father and grandfather had discussed the political situation years before and had decided to take steps. In 1939, my grandparents left Hungary "on vacation." They traveled to America and never returned to Budapest. The plan was for them to go on ahead and set up a life in the United States. My parents stayed behind, not knowing the atrocities that lay ahead in Europe. Knowing that my mother and grandmother would not want to be separated, they were not told of the plans, only of the "vacation." No one knew that later it would be impossible to escape Hungary. Ironically, my grandmother would become ill in New York. She died in 1942. By then escape from Hungary was impossible. My mother never saw her mother again. My father entered labor camp that same year.

During our months in hiding, whenever we saw a butterfly, my mother would tell me stories of my grandmother. The butterfly was our symbol of my grandmother watching over us. The stories gave us comfort and hope.

I was afraid of the air raids, of the loud noises and falling bombs. In October 1944, we packed to leave the Jewish House", our home—and went into hiding under assumed Gentile identities. At this point Jews were being rounded up and sent to camps. We were given Swedish passports by Raoul Wallenberg, and we considered using them. But when we went to the Wallenberg "safe house" my parents didn't feel safe and decided to take refuge with several Gentile acquaintances, who hid us in various basements and attics.

We lived for several months in an unfamiliar part of the city. We moved from place to place, trying to make ourselves invisible to the Germans, trying our best to stay hidden and safe.

I wanted to know where we were going to sleep. My mother told me that it wouldn't matter where we went, as long as we were together. I told her that I wanted to bring my pillow from our home. I stuffed it into my knapsack, and I cherished my one ordinary object from home, a constant object in my shifting, uncertain world. There was something so comforting about that pillow. To this day I travel with my pillow.

It must have been January 1945. The siege was coming to an end, but Budapest was still on the firing line between the Germans and the Allies. Now we were hiding from the Germans and the ongoing combat. There were dead bodies lying in the streets, all over the city, and even in the courtyard of the building, the basement of which was then our hiding place. It was bitter cold, and our shoes were worn out. I watched my father, a prosperous and respected business man, an intellectual, the man who bought me my first doll. After some hesitation, he left the relative safety of our basement hiding place, and ventured into the courtyard, pulling the boots off one body after another until our family was provided with new shoes.

Looking back over my war experiences, I believe that what protected me from the trauma of the horrible times was the loving care and shelter of my parents. Even lined up before a firing squad, my mother held me in her arms. She believed that if we died, we were going to do it together. I always knew with certainty she would never leave me alone.

The fact that we were able to stay together gave me a great sense of security.

Together with sadness, we found some joy.

Together with despair, we kept some hope.

Together with fear of the outside was the comfort of family.

New York 1952

Washington DC 2004

Name: Eva Cooper (née Eva Brust)

Born: Budapest, Hungary 1934

Paternal Grandparents	Maternal Grandparents
Grandfather	**Grandfather:**
Béla Brust	Adolf Schwarz
Place and date of birth unknown	**B**: Hungary, 1879
	D: New York,1958
Grandmother	**Grandmother:**
née Orova	Serena (née Deutsch)
Date and place of birth unknown	**B**: Hungary, 1887
	D: New York, 1942
Father	**Mother:**
Elek Brust	Livia (née Schwartz)
B: Budapest, 1900	**B**. Budapest, 1912
D: New York, 1957	**D**: New York, 2001

Prewar

I was born in Budapest and lived at 27 Erzsébet Kőrút. I went to Sziv utca elementary school and then to *Raskai-Lea leány gimnázium.* My father was in the wholesale paper business and a very prominent member of the Jewish community in Budapest. We belonged to the Dohány utca synagogue and lead a very privileged life until March 19, 1944, when the German army marched into and occupied Budapest.

War

We stayed in our apartment because our building had become a designated "Jewish House". Family and friends moved into all the rooms because only one room was allowed for each family. In October we went into hiding until the occupation in early 1945. We hid in attics, basements, and unoccupied apartments of kind people. In 1945, we returned to our old apartment, which needed a lot of work. It had been bombed and looted, but it was our home. My parents were busy looking for and identifying relatives and dealing with the loss of members of our family who had been killed in the camps.

Postwar

My father tried to rebuild his business, and my mother reopened my grandfather's watch company. However, within a year it was clear that the Communist Party was going to take charge, and all private businesses were now going to be "government controlled".

That is why my parents decided to emigrate to America, where my grandparents on my mother's side had already settled in 1939. We sailed for Dover, England, in the spring of 1947 and then to New York, where I have been living since. After arriving, I became an American teenager very quickly—I went to summer camp and then, in the fall, entered eighth grade on the Upper West Side. After junior high school, I was accepted at Hunter High School and continued at Hunter College, where I received my master's in special education. I married in 1955 and had a daughter in 1957. I was divorced and remarried almost twenty-eight years ago. I have a wonderful family that includes my daughter, Lisa Friedland, her husband, Ed, three stepchildren, Robin, Bruce and Jonathan and eight grandchildren, Adam, Peter, Andy, Emma, Nick, Daniel, Zoe and Jamie.

Budapest with brother Gyuri 1947

Suzanne Devorsetz

A Letter to My Grandchildren

Dearest Grandchildren—Sami, Lolly, and all those yet to come!

For those of us grandparents who are here through a miracle, we leave a history that we pass on to you and that you must pass on to your children and your children's children. We are grateful we were allowed the chance to produce other human beings for us to love and cherish and watch grow up.

Be responsible with the freedoms you enjoy, have joy in your life, and guard jealously the possibilities open to you.

I'm passing my memories onto you, since they are part of your legacy.

One of my earliest memories is witnessing my mother sewing the yellow star onto my nice navy blue coat, then being lined up in the courtyard (udvar) of our apartment house in Budapest where an Arrow Cross thug brutally ripped my gold necklace from my neck.

I remember my mother telling me that my name is no longer König Zsuzsi but Maria (I do not recall the last name) and being told not tell anybody my real name.

I remember being hidden by Christian friends behind a wall in their store and not being allowed to make any noise during the day. Their own two sons were Arrow Cross members, and fortunately they did not discover us.

I remember my mother stuffing a handkerchief into my mouth so no one should hear me while I had whooping cough, and removing it only when I was already turning blue and choking.

I remember my father and my uncle returning from "munkaszolgálat" (forced labor camp) and coming to get us out of the orphanage disguised as Nyilas. Father had overheard the Arrow Cross making plans to raid the orphanage and take the children to shoot them into the Danube. Many were sick and were left behind and suffered the terrible fate that we managed to escape.

I remember that after we were liberated and left the "Safe House", my mother cautioned us not to step on the dead bodies lining the street, still wearing the signature leather coats and boots of the Nyilas, while she herself gave them an occasional angry stomp.

I remember seeing the hungry populace carving up the carcasses of the dead horses in the street to make soup.

69

There was also a wonderful memory. In January 1945, Santa Claus showed up in Budapest in the guise of a Soviet soldier, one of our liberators, who loved children. He lifted me up and fed me. He proudly showed me his arm full of watches: watches that he had taken, probably at gunpoint (Zabrálta), from anyone who had one. Many of the Soviet soldiers came from remote areas in the Far East and had never seen a watch!

And a memory that stretches into the present!

The Germans had placed their ammunition storage in the building next to the orphanage where we were taking refuge so Allied bombers would avoid it. But they didn't count on the accuracy of the American pilots and their bombs; they blew up the ammunitions dump and didn't hit our building. However, the flames spread, and we all fled into the street. My mother stopped running, looked back, and cried out joyfully, "What a beautiful sight! Look, look!"* One of the other women shouted at her "Rozsi, are you crazy? You have two children with you, and you are stopping to look at a 'beautiful sight!'"

Many years later, my parents, your great grandparents, visited me in Syracuse and met a neighbor of ours who was in the U.S. Air Force. He told my parents that he was part of the bombardment team over Budapest. He said they had maps of where the Jewish children were, and they "knew that the Germans placed their ammunitions next to these buildings, of course." He was one of the navigators!

My mother thanked him for his accuracy and showed her appreciation with a huge hug.

I do not write these memories down to frighten you or make you sad, but to give you a glimpse into your history and your heritage, to help you understand how we became who we are and how we were able to survive the worst that can be done to us. But most of all, I write them down to impress upon you that, for all this to have been worthwhile, you have a duty to live your life to the fullest, to do your best to leave this world a better place than you found it, and most of all, to be proud of who you are.

All my love, Grandmother Zsuzsi

---

*See "War" in the following biography.

From Left: son Cary, Suzanne, son Marc, husband Sid, and son Andy
New York 2006

Letzte Meldung:

DIE LETZTEN GÄSTE des Festivals landeten heute nacht: Suzanne König und Ruth Lader, Stewardessen der israelischen Luftverkehrsgesellschaft El-Al, kamen aus Tel Aviv, um morgen an der Premiere des Israel-Dokumentarfilms „Paradies und Feuerofen" in der Film-Bühne Wien teilzunehmen. Regisseur Herbert Viktor, frischgebackener Bundesfilmpreisträger, begrüßte die hübschen Abgesandten.

BERLIN, 14. JAHR · Nr. 154   DIENSTAG, 7. JULI 1959   15 PFG. AUSWÄRTS 20 PFENNIG

The last guests to the festival landed tonight. Suzanna König and Ruth Lader, stewardesses on El Al Israeli Airlines arrived from Tel Aviv to participate in tomorrow's Premiere Presentation of the Israeli documentary "Paradies und Feuerofen" (Paradise and Fire Ovens) at the Film Bühne Wien. Herbert Viktor, producer of the documentary "Frischgebacken" (Freshly Baked), and recipient of the Federal Movie Prize, greeted the pretty envoys.

Name: Suzanne Devorsetz (née Zsuzsanna König)

Born: Budapest 1939

Paternal Grandparents	**Maternal Grandparents**
Grandfather	**Grandfather**
König. First name unknown	Károly Kocsis (Kohn)
B: Eisenstadt, Austria	**B:** Dunapentele, year unknown
D: Unknown	**D:** Auschwitz, 1944
Grandmother	**Grandmother**
Eugine (née Polak)	Nelly (née Kupfer)
B: Unknown	**B:** Fülöpszálas, year unknown
D: London, 1954	**D:** Munich, Germany, 1957
Father	**Mother**
Sándor König	Rozsi (née Kohn)
B: Eisenstadt, Austria, 1904	**B:** Fülöpszálas, Hungary, 1910
D: Vienna, 1992	**D:** Vienna, 2001

Prewar

My family was in the textile business. We lived at Csáki utca 36, in the Lipot Város section of Budapest. There were two children in the family, my older brother George and myself. We spent the summers vacationing in Balatonlelle, until the German occupation in 1944.

War

My father was conscripted in the *munkaszolgálat*. My mother, brother, and I went into hiding in Swiss and Swedish Houses and were even in the Ghetto for a while. *Somehow we ended up in an orphanage, but my mother and some other women were hired as cooks there, so she remained with us throughout. The cooking was done on the roof of the building, open to the elements. (See my story "Letter to my Grandchildren" for other details.)

Postwar

The war profoundly disrupted our lives. The Soviets were about to confiscate my father's business when we escaped from Hungary in 1948. We were able to do so because my father still worked at his knitting mill, and the needles for the machines were only available in England so he was able to get visas to leave the country. By 1948, my parents saw which way the wind was blowing and plotted on how to get out of the country permanently. My brother had been sent out to a school in Switzerland before the Iron Curtain came down, and my father asked the school to send an urgent message to my mother to say that he was very sick and she should come at once. When my mother requested her passport, she was told she could leave, but I had to stay behind. She had anticipated the circumstances and had coached me. I put on such a show of hysterics that the authorities immediately included me on my mother's passport. We all met in Vienna, and as we were getting off the train, a Serbian friend of ours who had been in the underground during the war was in another train, going back to Hungary. He shouted out through the window, *"Most megyek a nagymamaért!"* It meant, "I'm going to pick up grandmother!" And indeed he did. He smuggled her out in the trunk of his car!

My father was Austrian, so he was able to work in Austria, but when the Korean War started, mother became very nervous. There was still Soviet occupation in Austria, and she was afraid of a Third World War. She insisted on leaving Europe, but we couldn't get visa to the United States so we ended up in Australia. My brother and I loved it there, but our parents didn't. In 1955, we headed back to Europe, where I was put in boarding school in Paris. Our odyssey resulted in my eventually attending fourteen different schools in five different countries and being taught in four dissimilar languages.

My father, however, couldn't secure a work permit, so we proceeded to Germany, and I eventually ended up at the Dolmetcher Schule (Interpreter's School) in Munich, where I became a French-German translator. I worked for Lufthansa German airlines. I then moved to El Al, which eventually transferred me to New York in 1961. After I moved to New York, the El Al office where I had worked in Munich was blown up by explosives, and I lost a very dear friend.

To the Present

I met my husband in New York shortly after my arrival, and after we were married in 1961, we moved to Syracuse. In between raising three sons I started my own travel business.

My three sons are Marc (born 1962). He is on Wall Street. Andy (born in 1967) works in commercial real estate, and Cary (born in 1974) is a lawyer in Washington. We now have two grandchildren, Alexander Sami and Lolly-Rose, and we visit them in New York as often as possible. I love the theater, dance, sports, reading when time permits, and I have a great interest in world politics.

Greta, center, with her mother behind her, her aunt, and her siblings
Budapest 1944

Greta Elbogen

A Mother in 1939
On the run from Vienna to Csorna and Budapest

Why don't I remember sweet lullabies
Or soft words of love—adoration
From you, Mom?

Is this you with the harsh brush
Tackling chickenpox
On my little body in 1939?

Didn't you see my pretty face
My lovely body
My innocence
My glow?
Couldn't you just hold me once
Mother, with pride and joy?

Lullabies, yes.
Wouldn't it be nice.
But what I see is
Gripping fear in my mother's eyes.

WHERE IS MY TEDDY BEAR?

Hiding in a Red Cross Shelter

Where is my teddy bear?
Who dares to take my little bundle of clothes?
Who am I, what do I do?
Seven years old and all alone.
Many other children are
At this place.
I am just a number,
Not for real.

The room is cold.
I share a narrow bed
And there is only little cover in that.

A little bit of food
And nothing to drink.
Did I just sip from a can of urine?

MY BEAUTIFUL GRANDMOTHER

In memory of my dear grandmother, Leah Fischman,
who perished in Auschwitz

My beautiful grandmother,
You have such a special touch.
You put your shawl to heal my fears and such.

This well of love and tenderness
Had a very short stay for me
As we were separated
And you became one of the
Sacred flames of Auschwitz.

Thank you for the memories.
Thank you for your love.
I believe I owe you so much.

Greta with her first grandchild
New York 1982

Name: Greta Elbogen (née Grete Fischmann)

Born: Vienna, 1937

Paternal Grandparents	Maternal Grandparents
Grandfather	**Grandfather:**
Mano Fischman (Menachem, Mendl)	Siegmund Rechnitzer (Simon Jitzchok)
B: Unknown	**B:** Unknown
D: Csorna, Hungary, before WWII	**D:** Burgenland, Austria, 1922
Grandmother	**Grandmother:**
Hermine (née Kohlmann (Hendl)	Klara (née Deutsch Klerl)
B: Unknown	**B:** Unknown
D: Csorna, Hungary, before WWII	**D:** Burgenland, Austria, 1929
Step-grandmother:	
Leah Fischer	
B: Unknown	
D: Auschwitz, 1944	
Father:	**Mother:**
Nathan Fischman (Noson)	Ida (née Rechnitzer Chava)
B: Csorna, Hungary, 1902	**B:** Burgenland, Austria, 1902
D: Dachau concentration camp, 1945	**D:** Brooklyn, New York, 2006

Prewar

My parents married in 1929 in Frauenkirche in Burgenland, Austria, where my mother and her five siblings grew up. My father's family was originally from Csorna, Hungary. My parents settled in Vienna, where my father at the age of twenty-seven established a wholesale grain business with two of his brothers. My parents were practicing orthodox Jews and attended the well-known Schiff Schul (synagogue). They had four children between 1930 and 1937. I was the fourth child, born in 1937. Our lives were perfect. We had fine clothes and a lovely home. My parents were known to help the needy. In 1938, after the Anschluss, the annexation of Austria into Nazi Germany, my parents decided to flee to Hungary, where my father's stepmother, five siblings, and their families lived. The Austrian branch of the family was scattered in all directions.

War

From 1940 to 1942, my father briefly joined a business and we settled in Budapest. Our life seemed normal until my father was told to report to a forced labor camp. He was taken to many different slave labor camps. His final station was Dachau concentration camp in Germany, where he perished in 1945. My mother and my older sister survived in a Raoul Wallenberg–protected house in Budapest. My two older brothers and I were hidden in a Red Cross shelter on Budakeszi út on the outskirts of Budapest during the winter of 1944–45.

Postwar

There was no celebration in our family when the war ended. Our mother was so traumatized that we were immediately taken to a children's home. Later, my older brothers were sent to an orthodox Talmudic seminary in England. I grew up with my mother and sister with the support of the Jewish community in Budapest. My formal education began in third grade. While I attended elementary school I participated in a Jewish afternoon program at Dob utca 10. I studied at the all-girls Jewish *gimnázium* (high school) in Budapest from 1952–56. I believe that this fine institution nurtured and inspired me for life.

The Present

In 1956, we received our Austrian citizenship and returned to Vienna with lots of memories, no money, and no plans for the future. I, the youngest of four, decided to marry first. I married a Hungarian man who lived in New York, just to get away from my family and their helplessness. My marriage was a challenge. It forced me to find out who I was. After twenty years and raising four children I asked for a divorce. By then, I had completed my studies at Brooklyn College and had also received a master's of social work degree from Hunter College School of Social Work. The first position I requested was with a Holocaust victim's agency. My tragedies still continued after the war. I had already lost my father, my grandmother, and extended families during the war, but I also lost my two brothers to mental illness. One passed away in a nursing home in 1982. I adopted the eldest and still care for him in New York City.

I made many changes in my life. I worked as a social worker for fifteen years. Then I began to build my private practice in psychotherapy by continuing my education in related fields: family therapy and holistic forms of healing. I benefited from psychotherapy, too. Being involved in the arts of singing and dancing has made my life exciting. I see myself as a teacher who is able to help others by understanding the meaning of my own life experiences. I believe that all of us, if we choose, are able to leave behind the notion of being victims and can embrace life, living it to the fullest.

Budapest, circa 1943

Dr. Ivan Elkan

A Miraculous Escape

It was several months after the German occupation of Hungary on the 19th of March 1944, that this "Miraculous Escape" took place. My mother, my sister, who was five years my senior, and I, age 8, lived in a so-called "Protected House" (*védett ház*). The protection this house offered from the random and barbaric violence visited upon the wretched occupants was less real than perceived. Families of displaced Jews lived there in cramped quarters, sharing facilities with unknown fellow Jews. Ironically, we were thought to be the lucky ones.

Our father was in a labor battalion (*munkaszolgálat*). One day, when our mother left the building to try to secure his release—if even for a few days—our building was raided by the infamous Arrow Cross, who were often more atrocious than the German occupiers. They rounded up all the adult tenants, along with the children; they allowed only the old and sick, like our grandparents, who had managed to move in with us, to stay in their apartments.

We all had to make our way down to the courtyard, which seemed to be a very large area. (On a return visit to Hungary fifty years later, I visited the building where we had lived in Katona József utca, and to my great surprise, the courtyard was small and not as vast as I had remembered from my childhood.)

We were surrounded by members of the Arrow Cross, some as young as seventeen or eighteen, and all of them with guns hanging from their shoulders. They began to move the column of assembled Jews out of the building. Suddenly, my sister realized that, somehow, we had to prevent ourselves from being lead out of the courtyard.

She approached one of the Arrow Cross and started to pull at his sleeve, crying desperately and begging him to let her (and me) go back to our apartment to our grandparents. At first, he ignored my sister's pleas, but eventually, perhaps because he was annoyed by her persistent crying and pleading, shoved her aside and motioned to her and me that we could go back.

We didn't know that our mother had arrived back at the house just at the time of the raid. She was accompanied by a Gentile friend, who had often been very helpful with food, courage, and other assistance. When my mother saw the columns of Jews being led away from the house, guarded by a handful of young thugs with guns, wearing the notorious armband of white and red stripes with the arrow cross symbol in the middle, she had no doubt that her children were in great danger. Only the forceful persistence of her Gentile friend prevented her from entering the building to be with us. A short time later, as she stood outside witnessing the march of the hapless Jews into uncertainty, did she notice that an elderly lady who knew our family was signaling from a window, indicating to her that her children were upstairs and in relative safety.

Later that day, when the raid ended, our mother came upstairs to rejoin us, promising herself never to leave her children alone again. She kept her promise, and the three of us were never separated until Budapest was liberated by the Russians.

The fate of the Jews taken on that day from this "Protected House" was never really known. Many of them didn't return, most probably shot into the Danube, as so many other Jews had been.

This experience has remained in my conscience for over sixty years and may have given rise to my later belief that one's fate at times is determined by inherently insignificant, haphazard happenings, such as a thirteen-year-old girl's sudden decision to launch an emotional appeal to a ruthless enemy and his unusual and unexpected reaction to it. Most likely our survival was decided by this unrehearsed act of my sister's—two lives lived for another sixty years or more, rather than instant death at the bottom of the Danube.

The Unknown Woman

Another episode in our lives confirmed my belief in the potential significance of coincidence. My mother, my sister, and I were walking arm in arm down a well-known street in Budapest, wearing the obligatory yellow star. We noticed a group of Jews being led down the street by a few of the Arrow Cross, and so we quickly changed our direction. All of a sudden, out of nowhere, a woman appeared, stopped us, and dragged us through a heavy iron door, into the vestibule of an apartment building. She gave my mother a serious tongue-lashing concerning the foolishness of walking around with our yellow stars displayed while the Arrow Cross were arresting any Jewish people they could find in the street. Without waiting for an answer or excuse from Mother, she ripped the yellow stars from each of our coats, stuffed them into Mother's coat pocket, and disappeared just as she had appeared a minute before. Trembling, we left the building, and as we made our way home safely, we could observe how, indeed, Jews were being rounded up everywhere.

We had no idea who this woman was. Was she Jewish or Gentile? However, it is more than likely that she saved us from being caught in the web of trapped Jews and possibly from execution.

She was there, at the right place, the right time—just a lucky coincidence!

Medical Student in Toronto, 1957

Celebrating 71st birthday, Toronto

Name: Ivan Elkan

Born: Budapest, 1936

Paternal grandparents:	Maternal Grandparents
Grandfather:	**Grandfather**
Samu Elkan	Jenö Deutsch
B: Pincehely, 1863	**B:** Ercsi, 1878
D: 1944, place unknown	**D:** Budapest, 1945
Following deportation by the Hungarians/Germans	
Grandmother:	**Grandmother**
Karolina (née Singer)	Regina (née Stern)
B: 1869 place unknown	**B:** Tokol, 1887
D: Unknown, Kalocsa	**D:** Toronto, Canada, 1956
Father:	**Mother**
Tibor Elkan	Elizabeth (née Deutsch)
B: Kalocsa, 1903	**B:** Budapest, 1911
D: Toronto, 1979	

Prewar

I was born in Budapest in 1936. We were a middle class family of four—my parents, my sister, and I—living in the 7th district of Budapest in a comfortable, though not fancy, apartment on the second floor of a four-story building. My parents had a textile store not too far from our apartment where they both worked while we were at school. Earlier, in the 1930s, we had a nanny, but in the 1940s, there were just the four of us living in the apartment.

War

My father was taken into the labor battalion, and after the German occupation of Hungary in March 1944, my mother, my sister, and I were evicted from our apartment. We had to move into a designated Jewish house, where we stayed for several months. After October 15, 1944, under the leadership of Ferenc Szálasi, the fate of the Jews of Hungary took a sharp turn for the worse. Around this time, with the help of an honest and courageous Hungarian Gentile man, my mother managed to obtain false documents for the three of us. These papers transformed us overnight. We had new names and identities as refugees from Debrecen, one of the larger Hungarian cities. Actually, we had never been there, and this resulted in some close calls, like the time when our anti-Semitic landlords, who, of course, had no knowledge of our Jewish background, proposed to have us meet some friends of theirs from Debrecen.

We were liberated by the Russians around the middle of January. In June or July, my father returned from Mauthausen, where he had been liberated by the Americans in May 1945. There, he had contracted typhus fever and lost half of his body weight.

Postwar

Eventually, we were able to move back into our apartment, and soon after, my mother started up our previous business with the help of some friends. Several months of treatment helped my father recover, and he was able to join her.

Following the Communist takeover of Hungary during the postwar years, we decided to leave the country. In late December 1948, we crossed into Austria in the middle of the night, carrying all that we owned in our hands and on our backs. We lived in Austria for six months and then moved to Munich, Germany, where my parents established a new textile business while my sister and I attended high school. In 1952, I transferred to another high school in Switzerland, but I had to return to Munich a year later. I graduated in 1954 and then attended the University of Munich's medical school. In 1956, I transferred to the medical school in Toronto, Canada, and received my degree in 1961. Following my internship, I undertook postgraduate studies in Toronto and, subsequently, in St. Louis, Missouri, obtaining my specialty certificate in internal medicine and membership in the Royal College of Physicians and Surgeons of Canada in 1968.

I was in private practice in my specialty (with a subspecialty in nephrology) from 1968 until 2000, and I was on staff at two major hospitals in Toronto. I also taught medical students and house staff at both hospitals, and I had professorial rank at the University of Toronto, School of Medicine. I was active in political and social issues concerning the medical profession, and I served as president of the Toronto East Medical Association and as a director of the Ontario Medical Association.

I married in 1973 and divorced in 1985. I have no children.

To the present

I retired from medical practice and teaching in 2000, and I have enjoyed my retirement years to the fullest, satisfying my interests in the arts, film, wine tasting, computer science, and other events, all of which were put on the back burner during my years of active practice.

Eva, left, with sister Vera. Mezötúr 1941

Eva Fabry

A Journey to Remember

My family lived in Mezötúr, a small town in the Great Plains of Hungary (Alföld). The Jewish community was a small but integral part of the town and lived in relative harmony with the Catholics and Protestants there. My family was in the lumber business; we owned a large and successful concern founded by my father's father.

In 1940, my father, like the other able-bodied Jewish men, was conscripted to do forced labor, *munkaszolgálat*. Later, he was sent to the Russian front and never returned.

In 1944, a series of indignities were inflicted on the Jews. It was compulsory to wear the yellow star. Eventually, all the Jews were to leave their homes. We were relocated to a part of the town designated as the Jewish ghetto. We could take with us only a few belongings. Each family lived in a single room, and so my mother, two grandmothers, and one grandfather left our comfortable homes to move in together. Our world was being turned upside down.

Soon, worse was to come. All the inhabitants of the ghetto were herded onto trains, usually used to transport cattle, and taken to Szolnok, a large town where a huge collection camp was set up for the Jews of the region. My sister Vera and I, only five and seven years old respectively, were terrified and confused, and we missed our safe, warm homes. At the collection center, the group was divided into two. One half was sent directly to Auschwitz. The other half, selected at the collection center, was sent to farms in Austria. My family was fortunate to belong to this group. Once more we were packed into trains and sent to Andlersdorf in Austria. Since all the Austrian men were in the army, fighting alongside the Germans, the Jews in this transport were to do the heavy farm work. My mother and her mother, both strong, healthy women, together with the forty others who had been deported from the towns and villages near ours, worked every day in the fields. The home that we all shared was a single hay shed. My father's parents, elderly and in poor health, were unable to keep up with the work. We later found out they were taken to Bergen-Belsen in the by-now-too-familiar cattle cars. They never returned.

Our group was moved from farm to farm for many months. In the meantime, air raids became more frequent. Often, we had to run into underground bunkers in the middle of the night. We heard the people screaming as the bombs fell around us. I was terribly scared. For some strange reason, I got in the habit of wearing my white gloves. Somehow, they made me feel secure.

One day, we were told to get ready to move. First they transported us to Strasshof in Austria. We were again jammed into cattle cars with all the families who had been working on the Austrian farms in the area. The adults around me understood by then what was in store for us. My sister and I only knew that something awful was going on and that we were in grave danger. Once more, we were helplessly confined. The doors of the wagons were tightly locked. After the train had gone some distance, we were overwhelmed by the sound of airplanes overhead and of bombs exploding all around us. Locked in the train, there was panic, commotion, and screams. We thought the end was here. My grandmother threw herself on top of me, protecting me with her body, and my mother did the same for my sister.

After a long time there came a great silence. Suddenly, daylight filtered into the wagon. The guards had opened the doors. When we got out, we realized they were no longer there. Afraid of the approaching Russian troops, they fled, taking the food supply with them. The rails had been completely destroyed. There was no way our train could move anywhere. It was a miracle none of the wagons were hit. Or was it? Had the Allied forces carefully planned the bombing, knowing the content of these railway carriages? That's what some people in the group thought.

Then we saw Russian tanks in the distance. At the same time, we made another amazing discovery. Another train had been stranded nearby, a supply train filled with real food. My grandmother bravely joined the desperate men and women helping themselves to this windfall. She took as much as she could carry with her.

When the Russian soldiers reached our pathetic group, they were very friendly to us children. One of them even let me look through his binoculars. We were all taken on their tanks to a special camp in Pozsony. Here we were able to get washed and cleaned, and we soon started on our way back home, during the last gasps of World War II.

The fighting hadn't stopped. Battles were still going on. The Germans were shooting all around us. Dodging the gunfire, we walked at first, throwing away anything that weighed us down. At the end, we managed to ride on top of an open freight train toward Hungary. Fortunately, it did not rain and the weather was mild. It was the end of April.

Our first stop was in Budapest, where we found that some of our relatives were still alive. My grandmother, who had managed to save some of the bounty from the abandoned supply train, was now ready to share it. We, the deported, provided food for those who had just barely managed to survive in the city under siege. My grandmother was my great hero in those days.

When we finally arrived at our home in Mezötúr, we found our beautifully furnished house empty, looted, but intact. We slept on borrowed mattresses in the bare rooms.

Little by little, those of us who had survived began to get our lives together.

Budapest 1951   *New York 1967 with son Stephen*

Boston 2007 with Grandchildren, Madeline, Alex & Jonathan

Name: Eva Fabry (née Eva Szöke)

Born: Budapest 1936

Paternal Grandparents	Maternal Grandparents
Grandfather	**Grandfather**
Zsigmond Szöke	Béla Wohl
B: Szolnok, 1866	**B:** Unknown
D: Bergen-Belsen, 1945	**D:** Terbeled, Hungary, 1928
Grandmother	**Grandmother**
Ethel (née Ribner)	Iren (née Bindfeld)
B: Mezötúr, 1874	**B:** Place unknown, 1890
D: 1945, on the way home	**D:** Budapest, 1976
from Bergen-Belsen	
Father	**Mother**
István Szöke	Anna (née Wohl)
B: Mezötúr, 1905	**B:** Terbeled, 1914
D: The Russian front, 1943	**D:** Budapest, 2004

Prewar

My family lived in a small town called Mezötúr, a short distance from Budapest. My paternal grandfather had founded a lumber business, and my father became an important partner in it. It was a very lucrative, large firm with a special railway line connecting it to the main station of the town. We lived in a beautiful, big house, surrounded by a huge garden. We had a cook, a maid, a nanny, and a chauffeur. We took wonderful vacations. My younger sister and I had a loving, warm family life.

War

In 1942, my father was taken into a forced labor camp (*munkaszolgálat*) and later shipped to the Russian front. In 1944, the German army marched into Mezötúr. At first, we had to move into the ghetto, but soon after, we were deported by train, in wagons used for cattle, to a farm in Andlersdorf, Austria. There, my mother and grandmother had to do heavy farm work. Fortunately for us, my mother spoke fluent German, and so, by acting as interpreter for the group of Jewish deportees, she managed to make our lives more tolerable.

Postwar

My father did not return from the war. His parents had died in the concentration camp at Bergen-Belsen. Only his younger brother came back. He eventually married my mother and became a loving stepfather to my sister and me. In 1949, the Communists took over the business that we had started again, and we moved to Budapest. I went to a high school specializing in textile chemistry. In 1956, when the Hungarian Revolution began, I was a freshman at the Technical University of Budapest. I walked six hours in the snow to escape to Austria, received a British scholarship, and graduated from the University of London with a degree in chemistry. I married one of my classmates from Hungary in 1960, and we both immigrated to the United States a year later.

Life to the present

In April 1964, my son, Stephen, was born. After I received my master's degree in education, I became a science teacher. My husband and I divorced in 1967. I worked at Mt. Sinai Hospital, doing medical research, until 1983, when I became a real estate broker and am still busy discovering the chemistry of sellers and buyers. My son lives in Boston with his family, and I spend as much time as possible with my three wonderful grandchildren. I am involved with the spiritually oriented Pathwork Organization and do volunteer work for the New York City Opera and at the National Academy Museum in New York.

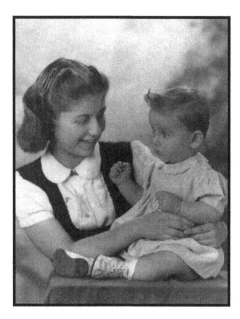

Budapest 1943, with Sister, Mari

Kathlin Feuerstein

Residual Memories

Someone once said to me, "You were just a baby, what do you know? You can't remember anything!"

It made me really angry!

True, I have no conscious recollection of the Holocaust experience, but the residual effects have dogged me all my life, like a subliminal message, constantly on the edge of my radar screen. Identity crisis and confusion were the stuff that my growing-up years was laced with. It took years of pain and analysis to sort out what caused me so much anxiety.

I was born in Budapest in 1943, thirteen months before the German occupation of Hungary in March 1944. The ensuing horrific events were related to me piecemeal over several years, as though they lacked relevance to my life.

My mother's terse account of the entire horrendous time was, "They shot at us. We hid. We had no sugar. What do you expect? It was war."

It seems that once the bombing raids started, and Jews were running from hiding place to hiding place, a baby was an added danger. Consequently, our housekeeper took me to her village, pretending that I was hers and that I had been born during her years of service in the city. My mother's somewhat reproachful account of that was also much abbreviated: "You cried hysterically when she took you away from me, but when you came back a few months later, you didn't even recognize me!"

I'm still puzzled as to why I was returned to Budapest. I heard that at some point people thought the danger had passed. Then in October 1944, when Szálasi's Arrow Cross regime took over, I joined my sister, who was thirteen years older than me and had been placed in a convent in the country, which was later relocated to Budapest. When the nuns heard that the Fascists were conducting raids looking for hidden Jewish children, they warned us and told us to leave. With the help of a decent superior, my father was allowed to come home from *munkaszolgálat* (forced labor), and the family was together during the siege of Budapest. We were liberated in January 1945. It was my sister's birthday, and she wished for a bucket of water all to herself! My second birthday was two weeks later, and I am told that my mother made a cake … with an egg. I still don't know where she found an egg!

After Liberation, life seemed to get back to normal—except that I could feel the vibrations of airplanes before anyone else could hear them, and I would yell at everyone to go into the bathroom (the safest place in the apartment), where I ended up with diarrhea. Being in the country terrified me.

Finally, in 1948, we came to the United States on a visitor's visa, with resident visas to Paraguay in my father's pocket. First we went to Cleveland and then settled in California in 1951. My parents had to present themselves every January as "aliens," and we were regularly warned that they could be deported. The first time I also had to go was when I turned twelve, and I panicked because authority figures have always terrified me, whether they wear uniforms or nuns' habits. My parents were allowed to stay as aliens through the good offices of a congressman, who "pork barreled" them onto a bill (now called a line-item). We did not get on track for citizenship until 1956, when Hungarians were granted political amnesty as a result of the revolution. I got my citizenship separately when I was eighteen.

I experienced a major panic attack on my honeymoon, when, not only were we "in the country" in Yosemite National Park , but I caught sight of two nuns sitting at a nearby table. I dropped out of college and went into therapy. A couple of years later, pregnant with my first child, we moved to Connecticut, where my husband had managed to rent a home in a quiet adult community in rural Woodbury. Again, big trees, country, no people ... panic attacks! I took out the telephone directory and looked up art classes, rabbis, and therapists, then found an apartment where there were lots of people with children around. Therapy continued.

I had to learn to separate myself from my children, not physically, but by letting them grow up to be individual human beings who did not have to share my experiences and who did not have to have the fears, the anxiety, the panic passed onto them but were allowed to develop into their own separate selves. Oh, the terrible, awesome responsibility of having children and keeping them safe—sometimes even from ourselves!

It's an ongoing process. I'm still trying to make sense of where I belong and who I am—all while ugly unremembered memories still occasionally rear their ugly heads.

Los Angeles 1961

New York 2006

Los Angeles 2007, Mother's 100th birthday party, Sister Mari (left)

Name: Kathlin Feuerstein, (née Katalin Kahan)

Born: Budapest, 1943

Paternal Grandparents	Maternal Grandparents
Grandfather	**Grandfather**
Aaron Kahan	Károly Berkovits
B: Munkács, 1880 (?)	**B**: Mármarossziget, cc 1878
D: Budapest, 1960	**D**: Budapest, 1914
Grandmother	**Grandmother**
Berta (née Marguliesz)	Hani (née Reisman)
B: Unknown	**B**: Ungvár (?), 1886
D: Budapest, 1951	**D**: Los Angeles, 1970
Father	**Mother**
Jenö Kahan	Gizella (née Berkovitz)
B: Munkács, 1908	**B:** Budapest, 1907
D: Palm Springs, California, 1993	**D:** Los Angeles, 2007

Prewar:

The Kahans lived quite comfortably, in a roomy apartment. The grandparents kept a kosher home, but were modern Orthodox. Grandpa (paternal) was on the road a lot. He was a salesman, but he was always home for the Friday family dinner.

My maternal grandpa was a salesman, with an exclusive for Hungary for Hectograph machines, an early repro system for use mostly by restaurants. He married grandma against his parents' wishes (she had no dowry). She was a working girl at age fourteen, a secretary with typing and shorthand skills that she learned for free from the first store selling Smith Corona typewriters in Budapest. They had to provide someone who could use their product when they sold a typewriter. She worked for Shell Oil and a lawyer. When they married, they started a business with the Hectograph distributorship and other paper products for use in restaurants and businesses. The family lived in the back of the store, with grandpa on the road, grandma working the store, and grandma's mom, Alexandra Maria, minding the three kids and household.

Grandpa died in 1914 of pneumonia, just before World War I.

Grandma continued the business. She started to manufacture paper products in the early 1920s in a rental facility in Sip utca and ran a wholesale retail store for restaurant and business supplies and paper products in Sip utca 4. By then, life was much more comfortable, with a nice apartment on Rákoczy ut.

She moved the manufacturing part into her own building around 1935. At this time, she produced many other products, like paper napkins, toilet paper, paper cups, trays, containers, and disposable paper spools for the textile mills. There were well over one hundred employees, maybe as many as two hundred (my older sister can't remember). For a while the family lived in the factory building to help with finances, but in a year they moved to a very nice suburban apartment on Stefania ut. I understand that life was very comfortable.

My mother and father met at a dance in the summer of 1936 in Mátyásföld, where the family was renting a summerhouse. At the time, dad was a salesman for house wares, and mom was separated from her first husband. In 1929, she had married a stockbroker, and my sister was born in 1930, but by around 1932, the marriage had come apart. My parents dated in secret for several years until her divorce became final and they were able to marry.

War

I was born in the last year of the war and have no conscious memory. See my story.

Postwar

Things got a lot better after the war. My family went back into business, and life seemed normal. But then, Mother started to go to auctions exchanging money for household goods. In March 1948, we went to Prague with a group. In the synagogue, someone said to my father, "You are supposed to be smart, a Kahan. Why are you still in Budapest?" That was the weekend Jan Masaryk was murdered by the Soviets by being thrown out of a window. By June, we had left Hungary. Mother collected all those household goods in lieu of money, which we couldn't bring out. We came to the United States on visitors' visas—to Cleveland, although we had visas to Paraguay. Eventually we moved to California. I started school there, later going to Berkeley and UCLA.

Life to the Present

I got married at twenty, while still in college, and I had two children and continued to live in California. I was divorced in 1976. I worked for my father in contract importing and mass merchandising sales in houseware items. I traveled widely to the Orient and the Philippines and directed national sales. We worked with Sears Roebuck, JC Penney, and many of the discount chains.

I got remarried in 1980 and moved to New York in 1983, where I have lived ever since. My passion is ice-skating, which I continue to do. I love to dance, travel, and most of all, see my family: my husband Phil; my sons, David and Benjamin, and their wives Tiffany and Yona; my grandchildren, Elijah, Olivia, Arella, Adrian, and Mariposa; my stepchildren, Jon and Jennifer Feuerstein; and of course, most specially, my sister Mari, who not only gave me my name but without whom I probably would not be here today.

Budapest 1940

Susan Gerey

Escape on New Year's Eve

My father was in a labor unit (*munkaszolgálat)*, in 1944. Since he was in charge of food supplies, he could leave the Ferihegyi Airport, where his unit was stationed to work, to get more provisions for the camp in Budapest. Luckily, he had a driver's license, so he was the one to drive the truck from the airport, located at some distance, to the city, hence he was occasionally able to visit my mother and me. We were still living in our own apartment, which was in a protected house. I was eight years old.

One day, news reached my father that all the Jews who lived in protected houses were to be moved to a ghetto in Dohány utca, where the main synagogue of Budapest was located. He managed to get false identity documents for us. Our family name changed from Márkus, suggesting Jewish ancestry, to Horváth, a reliable Hungarian Gentile surname. We moved into the ghetto under this name as Christians, that is, as Jews who had converted. For this reason, the compulsory star we had to sew on our clothing was white, not yellow, as for other Jews. When it became obvious that not even our privileged status could protect us, my father found us a hiding place in the home of a Christian family. My mother and I lived in the tiny maid's room off the kitchen. I don't remember the address. It was on the Pest side of the city, near the Danube River.

On December 31, 1944, I became very sick with a bad cold and fever. To prevent her from getting my cold (we only had one narrow bed), my mother slept in the kitchen that night while I stayed in the maid's room. All of a sudden, two *Nyilas* burst into the kitchen looking for Jews and questioned my mother. First of all, they wanted to know why she had an accent in Hungarian. They accepted the reason—which happened to be true—that my mother was born in Czechoslovakia. She answered all their other questions concerning her ethnic origin and religion seemingly to their satisfaction. Then they came into the room where I was lying in bed, refusing to allow my mother to accompany them.

They asked me my name, and I answered, "Horváth Zsuzsika," keeping in mind my new false identity.

Then they tricked me. "Your mother told me everything about you. There is just one thing she forgot to tell us. Did you wear a yellow or white star?"

"A white star," I said, not realizing that with this answer I was betraying us. Conversion to Catholicism was no protection for anyone born a Jew.

The two *Nyilas* brought me into the kitchen, where they berated my mother for having lied to them. Bragging that they had just shot eleven Jews into the Danube, they assured us that we would be the twelfth and the thirteenth.

Somehow, my mother had the presence of mind to offer them packages of cigarettes. She never smoked, so I wondered why she had some. Of course, cigarettes served as currency to buy necessary things and also as bribes in the days when money had lost its value. By then, sounds of battle could be heard clearly, even the rumble of the Russian tanks. The *Nyilas* took the cigarettes and, promising to spare us, asked my mother if she would come forward to testify on their behalf once the Russians arrived and they were tried as war criminals. Even though my mother agreed to this bargain, we would still have to leave the apartment, they said. She could not move a sick child, my mother insisted, and she threatened to have us both take poison rather than go. We were allowed to stay for the time being and watched them leave with relief.

An hour later they were back. They assured us that they had found a safe hiding place for us. Trusting—what else could we do?—we followed the two men along the Dunapart, or the bank of the Danube, to a large abandoned paper factory owned by Sass and Bauer (I still remember the name of the company). We were to hide in one of the giant empty crates used to store bales of paper. Then they left. Suddenly we heard a scream, *"Márkus néni!"* ("Auntie Márkus!"). A voice called to my mother, using her real last name. All older women are called "auntie" in Hungarian. A head popped up. It was the Jewish tenant from the sixth floor of our old building. We then realized that families of Jews were hiding in every crate in the huge empty space. We stayed there till it was safe to come out. The Germans had finally been defeated.

It was only later we found out that the apartment where we had hidden in the maid's room off the kitchen was bombed the night we left, and the whole building was totally leveled.

My son insists I am a true survivor. My time to die, I suppose, had not yet come that night.

1970

New York 2005

With mother, New York, 1989

112

Name: Susan Gerey (née Zsuzsanna Márkus)

Born: Budapest 1935

Paternal Grandparents
Grandfather
Mano Márkus
B: Ujpest, year unknown
D: Budapest, 1948

Grandmother
Esther (Née Tolnay, sister of Simon Tolnay owner and publisher *Tolnai Világlapja*)
B: Brno, year unknown
D: Budapest, 1948

Father
Dénes Márkus
B: Ujpest, 1904
D: New York, 1965

Maternal Grandparents
Grandfather:
Leopold Lavezky
B: Brno, year unknown
D: Auschwitz, 1944

Grandmother
Adel (née Fischl)
B: Unknown
D: Auschwitz, 1944

Mother
Jeannette(née Lavezky)
B: Brno, 1909
D: New York, 1998

Early Life

I was born in Budapest, where my father owned the Windsor Toothbrush Factory. I was seven years old and in first grade in the Skót Iskola (the Scottish School) when the air raids started and the Germans occupied Hungary. When the *Nyilas* started to hunt Jews, we had to wear a yellow star.

War

My mother and I hid with false identification papers with a Gentile family. On New Year's Eve, the *Nyilas* discovered us in our hiding place, took us to the Danube, and were ready to shoot us into the river, but my mother managed to save us (see my story). My father was taken to a forced labor camp and then to the concentration camp at Mauthhausen. He survived this terrible ordeal and came back to us after the war.

Postwar:

During the Communist regime, I attended the *Bajza utcai Gimnázium* (middle school). I continued my education at the *Mária Terézia Gimnázium* (high school), from which I graduated in 1954. My brother, Peter, was born in 1947. In 1965, during the Hungarian Revolution, my parents, brother, and fiancé and I escaped to Austria from Budapest, arriving in Vienna on December 21, 1956. There, Robert Gerey and I got married. We arrived in New York on the twenty-ninth of December and went to live in Jacksonville, Florida. In 1957, my son, Tommy, was born in Florida. We moved back to New York in 1959, where I studied at the Mayer School of Fashion, graduating with a diploma in design. From 1965 to 1984, I worked as a dress designer. My husband was a mechanical engineer. He passed away in 1982 after a short illness. My son is now married and lives in Arizona.

Marianna with mother, father and grandmother in 1947

Marianna Gersch

HOLOCAUST ODYSSEY

We lived in Debrecen, the second largest city in Hungary. I was almost five years old when the Germans occupied Hungary on March 19, 1944. We were all rounded up to go to the Ghetto. My mother had a friend who lived there, and she allowed us to move in with her. From there, we were taken to the *Téglagyár*, the brick factory, where we were supposed to wait to be taken east presumably to work camps. The whole family was there: children, parents, grandparents, uncles, aunts, cousins. It was still very cold, yet we were all outdoors as there was no interior space. One of my cousins had a newborn baby, who died there of pneumonia when it was only six weeks old.

There were three trains waiting for us. My uncle and his family were slated to go in train number three, while we were on the list for number two. My uncle, Sándor Bácsi, begged my father to bribe one of the Germans to change our train number so we could all be together, but my father refused to speak to the Germans, so we got on separate trains. It seems that the first and third trains went straight to Auschwitz and very few survived.

Our train headed east until it suddenly stopped, and after a while, it reversed its course and ended up going west. The train tracks going east had been bombed, and the train could not proceed. We ended up in Austria in a place called Strasshof, which was a sorting camp. From there, they sent people to various forced labor camps or death camps. My father was sent to Treiskirchen, a camp with slave laborers where he spent his time digging ditches, while we ended up in a place called Lobo on the outskirts of Vienna. There were two camps there, and we were terrified we would be separated, but the camp commandant surprised us, saying, "You are in Austria. You have nothing to fear."

He was indeed an astonishing man, certainly qualifying for "Righteous" status. Unfortunately, I don't remember his name. He made sure that the children were given milk, watered down though it was, and he actually managed to get my father to join us after my mother begged him to do so. However, the other Germans had big dogs and wore guns, and these two things frightened me horribly.

There was very little food in the camp. Our main staple was a soup made from the dregs of beets that had had the sugar pressed out of them. My mother often managed to scrounge potato peels from the officers' garbage bins, and she cooked them over a small fire that she made and which was surrounded by bricks to form a primitive stove.

The adults worked at cleaning and transporting bricks or cleaning officers' quarters, while the kids wandered around with not much to do. Sometimes we drew pictures in the dirt with sticks or played quiet games near our barracks.

Lobo had an oil refinery, which was a target for Allied bombs. It was one of my most terrifying experiences. Whenever the bombs came, we were rushed to the underground dirt shelters in the camp and had to lie there until the raid was over. But sometimes we didn't have time to get to the shelters and took refuge under trees as the bombs fell around us.

At some point during the wintertime, when it was very cold, we were transferred to a work camp in Wiener-Neustadt. There was no heat, and there were days when we children didn't want to get out of bed because of the cold. My uncle Joseph caught pneumonia and died in a hospital. I remember there was a teacher from Debrecen there who taught us a little German and made sure we knew our address in case we got lost in the camp. I remember that it was Auhofstrasse, but I can't remember the number.

We were transferred to a place called Solinau for a while, where we lived in trailers and I remember it was very cold. Then we were taken back to Strasshof to be shipped to Bergen-Belsen. However, the train didn't even start to move because there was an air raid. Two of the cars were hit, and everyone in them perished. We were terrified. My grandmother prayed with me. My grandmother said, "Pray! God listens to children." We prayed, *"Ana Hashem Hosiah Na, Ana Hashem Hatzlicah Na,"* which means, "G-d, please save us. G-d, please rescue us!"

The Germans then came and opened our doors and told us to go back to the barracks, and then they disappeared. The Russians came and "liberated" us a few days later.

Before the Soviets arrived, we broke into the food storage areas, where my mother found a barrel with jam in the bottom that she scraped out. She came back covered in jam. My father found some boots that he kept — hoping to trade later for food. But as soon as the Russians arrived one soldier came, saw the boots, and said in Hungarian, *"Csizma. Ide!"* meaning, "Boots. Here!"

Grandmother boiled down the jam until it became the consistency of cheese so we could take it with us on our journey home. My father found a wagon, and somebody found a lame horse. We teamed up and we started off toward Hungary and home to see who had survived. The lame horse died on the way. We arrived in Budapest on VE Day. I particularly remember it because it was my grandmother's birthday, and everybody was yelling and screaming that the war was over.

We found our way back to Debrecen and learned that the Nazis had murdered most of our relatives. Fortunately, my parents, grandmother, and I survived and started our lives anew. Eventually, we came to America.

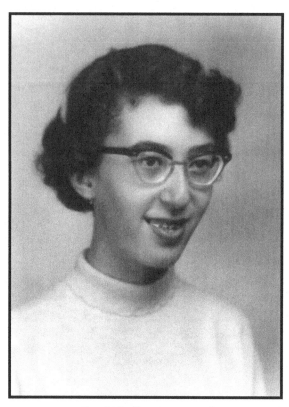

Little Falls NY, Age 16

New York City 2007

Name: Marianna Gersch (née Marianna Grünberger)

Born: Debrecen, Hungary, 1939

Paternal Grandparents	Maternal Grandparents
Grandfather	**Grandfather**
Adolf Grünberger	Albert Lövenheim
B: Hajduboszolo, Hungary, 1843	**B:** Debrecen, 1861
D: Hajduboszolo, 1921	**D:** Debrecen, 1914
Grandmother	**Grandmother**
Szidonia (née Lövenheim)	Ilona (née Grünberger)
B: Debrecen, 1854	**B:** Hajduboszolo, 1878
D: Hajduboszolo, 1904	**D:** New York City, 1960
Father	**Mother**
Jacob Grünberger	Helen (née Lövenheim)
B: Hajduboszolo, 1890	**B:** Amsterdam, New York, US, 1904
D: New York City, 1984	**D:** New York City, 1984

Prewar

I was an only child. My parents were part of a large, extended, middle-class family. My father was a lawyer, and my mother a milliner. She had a thriving business and employed several young women. My maternal grandmother, Ilona, lived with us. Our housekeeper, Dora Néni, was like a second grandmother and a part of our family for twenty-three years. We lived in a spacious four-room apartment with beautiful furniture, Persian rugs, and chandeliers. My early childhood was pretty normal. I attended nursery school and played with friends.

War

My earliest memories of the war were of the air raids when we had to run down to the cellar, sometimes staying there all night. I also remember my parents and my grandmother huddled around the radio, listening to Voice of America. My happy childhood ended before I was five years old in March 1944 when the German army marched into Hungary. We were soon herded into the ghetto, then the brick factory, and finally to several concentration camps. We were among the "lucky" ones who ended up in Austria. Most of my aunts, uncles, and cousins ended up in Auschwitz and were murdered there. We were in Lobo, near Vienna, where there was an oil refinery, and the Allies bombed it day and night. We were in several other camps in Austria, where my parents and even my grandmother had to work. Near the end of the war, we were in Strasshoff in a train wagon about to be taken to Bergen-Belsen and certain death when an air raid bombed the train and the tracks. We were ordered back to the barracks, and then the Germans disappeared. Two or three days later, the Soviets liberated us.

Postwar

After the war, we returned to Hungary to find out who from our large family was still alive. We very sadly found out that most of our relatives had been slaughtered in Auschwitz. We tried to put our lives back together in Debrecen, but thought that we should go to America. My father started his law practice again, working for barter since Hungarian money was worthless. My mother had lost all of her materials and equipment and did not start her business again. I started school and attended the Jewish school for four years. I came to the United States with my grandmother in 1949, when I was ten years old. We lived with my maternal uncle Jerome and his family in Little Falls, New York. My parents got stuck in Communist Hungary. They were finally able to join us in 1958 and settled in New York City.

Life to the Present

I came to New York City when I was eighteen and have lived here ever since. I went to nursing school and became a registered nurse. I married Charles E. Gersch in 1963. We have three wonderful children—Alan, Jonathan, and Jennifer—a wonderful daughter-in-law, Lili, and an adorable grandson, Jacob. I have worked in various nursing positions over the years. Currently, I am working as an adjunct professor, teaching nursing students one day a week.

I am grateful for having survived the Holocaust, and although I was not a Hidden Child, I feel privileged to be part of this group and honored to be asked to participate in this important project.

Munkács 1941

Judith Gertler

HAVE A U.S. PASSPORT, WILL IT SAVE ME?

It was mid-December 1944 when we arrived at an ancient fort on the outskirts of Komárom. The fort was built in the form of a star and called "Csillag Erőd". The place wore the battle scars of many centuries. The weather was horrendous, with snow and sleet falling all the way since we had left Budapest on this Death March*. The roads were icy and slushy. Our feet were frozen and tired as we were ushered into this huge labyrinth with no windows or electric lights. It was actually a basement storage area for animal feed.

Some straw was spread on the ground. We collapsed into this space, in wet clothing, one next to the other to keep our bodies warm. By the door at the entrance, were provided a pail for drinking water and another for our hygienic needs. We had no belongings, as we had dropped everything on the long way, to be able to keep up with the march. Our guards, members of the Hungarian Arrow Cross, or *Nyilas*, party, chased us with their dogs and rifles toward the German border.

Prior to the Death March, our group was kept under the protection of the Swiss consul. The Germans respected this for some time, hoping to exchange us for German prisoners of war. Then one day they collected all the common criminals who were imprisoned in the city, and we were attached to that unholy transport, called the *Tolonc* (vagrant persons). The language and the behavior of this crowd was shocking to my innocent ears. They were brutal, angry people, abusive to each other. I clung to my Aunt Mariska and couldn't get my thoughts together.

My mother had been with us until the night before we arrived at our stopping place in Komárom, and now she was missing. I looked for her and asked my aunt why she and my mother were no longer together. The guards had taken us children out of the line and placed us on horse-drawn carts nearby. My aunt explained that I was on one of the carts when my mother, unable to keep up with the march, stayed behind. The Arrow Cross guards had urged those who walked badly to rest by the road. They reassured them that the carts would come to pick them up, as they did with the children.

The cart that I had been placed on was at the end of the marching column, and I saw people who couldn't walk being escorted toward the bushes and shot from the back. I couldn't believe my mother might have been among them. I was hoping that she was on a cart, and I waited anxiously for her arrival. Days passed while we stayed in that dark fortress. Then December 20,

1944, my eleventh birthday arrived. I was very sad and demanded in my sorrow an explanation from my aunt. Why didn't she hold on to my mother?

My mother had saved me in the ghetto of Munkács from deportation to Auschwitz. She was a U.S. citizen with a valid passport, and that gave us the opportunity to be protected by the Swiss consulate. My mother, my aunt who had lived in Budapest, and I remained in a Swiss "protected house" until we were deported in spite of the promised protection.

In her youth, my mother had emigrated from Hungary to the United States and lived in New York for eleven years. With the Depression, she lost her job and decided to visit her family in Munkács. At that time, Munkács belonged to Czechoslovakia, but it was later returned to Hungary. Upon arriving there, she was introduced to an eligible, handsome young man. Love conquered her desire to return to the United States.

When the war broke out, my mother's first thought was to return to New York. The American Consul had advised her to purchase the necessary tickets and leave Europe immediately. We sold our home, shipped some of our belongings, and gave Grandma the furniture. Meanwhile, there were changes in the immigration laws, and the latest decrees specified that my mother could go alone immediately, but her child and husband would have to wait three months to follow. My mother was unable to commit herself to that separation. Thus we remained trapped in the war with rest of the Jews of Munkács.

From the fort of "Csillag Erőd", as the Germans had their trains available, they transported us to Rawensbrück, a women's camp in Germany. We arrived there on January 7, 1945, and suffered for months the atrocities and brutality of a concentration camp. We had to endure a second Death March when Rawensbrück was evacuated, all along being strafed by the airplanes above us. The Germans chased us out of the camp, saying it would be blown up but actually hoping we would all perish on the march to nowhere. At one point, we found ourselves in a forest that was on fire. The planes were targeting not only us, but the whole moving crowd, as we were marching with a motley collection of soldiers and civilians. All of Germany was trying to flee from the Allies, who were winning the war. To escape from the bullets, we had to hide in ditches until the planes passed. Our desperate march continued until the end of the war, when we were liberated by the Red Army to return to a much-changed home.

The American passport was sewn into my coat's lining, even as my mother and I separated. When the coat was taken away from me in the camp, it marked the end of the saga of my U.S. protection and only the memory of my mother remained.

See Glossary

Brooklyn NY 1967

Brooklyn NY 2007

Name: Judith Gertler, (née Judit Rosner)

Born: 1933, Munkacevo, Czechoslovakia.

Paternal Grandparents
Grandfather
Herman Rosner
B: Munkács, date unknown
D: Munkács, 1939

Grandmother
Odze Rezsi
B: Sátoraljaujhely, 1880
D: Auschwitz, 1944

Father:
Zoltan Rosner
B: Munkács   1906
D: Israel, 1980

Maternal Grandparents
Grandfather
S'Maya Klein
B: Szeredne, date unknown
D: Beregszentmiklos, 1916
(Spanish flu pandemic)

Grandmother
Sara Hana (née Feldman)
B Beregszentmiklos, date unknown
D: Beregszentmiklos, 1916
(Spanish flu pandemic)

Mother
Marian (née Klein)
B: Beregszentmiklos, 1904
D..December 1944 (Shot by the
Nyilas on death march)

Prewar

My father was a manager in a hardware company, and we lived in middle-class comfort. I attended a private Hebrew school.

War

In 1941, my father was called up for forced labor *(munkaszolgálat)*. He served on different fronts, but he was allowed to visit us several times. My mother carried on as best she could, keeping close ties with my grandmother and my father's siblings.

In 1944, when the Jews were assembled in the ghetto and put into cattle cars for deportation to Auschwitz, my mother pulled out her American passport, and miraculously, they honored it. We were under Hungarian security protection until we were transferred to Festetics utca in Budapest, which was a Safe House under the protection of the Swisss and we were hoping to be liberated there. But Mr. Carl Lutz didn't rescue us. On December 11, 1944, our destiny changed for the worse. (See my story.)

Postwar

The Red Army liberated us. We had been hiding on a farm, having escaped the Death March, and we were anxious to find a DP camp in order to be shipped home. But the map of Europe had changed, and Munkács had become part of the Soviet Union, so we were mistaken for returning Russians who had escaped during the war, and consequently, we were mistreated by the liberating Soviets. Finally, after lengthy explanations by my aunt Mariska, who had had Russian schooling, we were able to get to Munkács. My father had survived and was looking for us in Czechoslovakia. When we were finally reunited, he took us to Prague to escape the Russians. I was sick and hospitalized for a long time. With the threat of being sent to Russia hanging over us, my father decided to take me to the Zionists. While traveling to Palestine illegally, I was detained by the British and sent to Cyprus. After arriving in Israel (Palestine at the time) in September 1947, I attended the agricultural school of Ben Shemen for three years and served two years in the army. My father remarried, and I worked with my stepmother Manci after studying at the Teacher's Seminary.

Life to the Present

I visited the United States in 1957 and met my husband, Harry. We were married in 1959 and settled in a Jewish area in Brooklyn. A year later, my only son, Marc, was born. Marc received a Jewish education then went on to college at Columbia University and to Boston Law School. When he graduated, he said, "Now you go to college!" and I did. I received my bachelor's of arts in history from Touro College in 1984. I enjoyed studying. I love to attend college lectures and go to book clubs and other cultural activities.

In 1991, I went to the First International Conference for the Hidden Child and was a founding member of HHC. We travel frequently to Israel to see family, and they too visit us often.

Noordwijk Holland 1937
Hans with Mother

Hans Gesell

FOOD FROM THE SKY

On May 10th 1940, the German army attacked Holland. This came as a surprise to the Dutch, who had hoped to remain neutral, as they had in WWI. Dutch marines prepared to blow up the Rhine river bridges to slow the German advance. The Germans countered with an ultimatum: "Surrender or we will destroy Rotterdam."

The bombardment began on a bright sunny day. It was May 14th 1940. I was five years old and at home with my parents and our Hungarian maid, Terci. We lived on the fifth floor of a modern, twelve-story building, then the tallest in Rotterdam. Our wrap-around windows were above the rooftops of the neighborhood, and we had a panoramic view toward the center of town where the great harbor lay.

The bombers came in waves—initially they dropped explosives that brought down buildings and destroyed the harbor facilities. Next came incendiaries, which set the heart of the city on fire. The residents of our building hid in the basement during the attack. By nightfall, when the planes stopped coming, my father put us in his car and drove to the home of a friend in the suburbs. Flames were raging all around us—even the hospital across the street had been hit—but our building had been spared.

The following day, we returned home and prepared to live under the German occupation. Although my mother's parents in Hungary and my father's father in Holland were all Jewish, my parents decided not to register when the order was issued. My father had changed his name to Gesell, his mother's maiden name, shortly after WWI, and my mother received false papers from her sister in Budapest. Three of the four grandparents had died long before the war. Only my father's mother, Antonia Gesell, survived until 1945. We had no religious affiliation of any sort.

In 1942, the Germans built camp Westerbork on the Dutch-German border, and the deportation of Dutch Jews began. Soon there were no more yellow stars to be seen on the street. Those who escaped the net were in hiding. Eventually 140,000 Dutch Jews were deported. Only thirty thousand survived the war.

The occupiers' next move was to round up men between sixteen and forty years of age to work as forced laborers in German factories. Since many men refused to report, the German army would conduct frequent raids called *razzias* during which city blocks were cordoned off and house-to-house searches were conducted. These were frightening times.

Our building was heated by steam, which was supplied by a central plant. By 1943, the plant was shut down as all available coal was shipped to Germany. Gas and electricity were soon shut off, too, and so the modern appliances were removed and replaced with wood-burning stoves. Candles, kerosene lamps, and carbide lights lit our apartment.

Each night, plywood covers were placed over all windows to maintain a total blackout, and no one was allowed out at night after eight at night unless they had a special permit. The two elevators in our building were removed, and the empty shafts were used to haul up buckets of water and other supplies to the twelve floors of apartments. German soldiers occupied the roof of our building because it overlooked most of the city. A lookout was constructed there and linked by telephone to an anti aircraft battery in a park nearby. Yet when the *razzias* were on, our Hungarian friend, George Steiner, would escape the dragnet by hiding in the bottom of the elevator shaft.

By 1944, food had become extremely scarce. Ration cards were meaningless because store shelves were empty. Farmers grew crops and kept cattle and fowl, but 90 percent of farm products were shipped to Germany. By the winter of 1944, a great wave of hunger swept across Holland, eventually killing thirty thousand people. By this time our diet had been reduced to sugar beets and tulip bulbs. Most people survived on less than a thousand calories per day. Those who could, would venture out of the cities on bicycles in search of food, stopping at farmhouses and trading the family silver for a bag of potatoes.

I was then nine years old and in the third grade of elementary school. My friends and I played in the street like any normal boys our age, except that when we roughhoused and fell or scraped our knees, the wounds would turn into ulcers due to lack of nutrition.

Children from the "blue-collar" streets near us, dressed in rags over skin and bones, would often ring our doorbell and beg for food. My mother never turned any away, in spite of my father's grumbling. When we did eat, the assault on our digestive tracts frequently resulted in agonizing abdominal pains. The winter was extremely harsh, and people were desperate. Men would sometimes injure themselves to gain admission to a hospital in the hope of getting some food.

Then, at the end of April 1945, a miracle occurred: the Red Cross announced that food would be dropped from airplanes over various parts of Holland. The Germans knew the end of the war was near, and they allowed Royal Air Force planes to fly over Rotterdam on April 29th 1945. For the first time since 1940, we were allowed onto the roof of our building, as the German lookouts had disappeared, leaving their little fortified bunker behind. We stood and waved as each huge plane—they were Lancaster bombers with big red crosses painted on their sides—flew over us so close that we could see the pilots through the glass canopies. It seemed to me that they waved back.

We cheered as the boxes dropped down from the bomb bays over the outskirts of Rotterdam. There, the food was gathered and sorted by the members of the Dutch Resistance. A day or so later, our share arrived at our front door. We each received a loaf of bread, a stick of margarine and a small box of graham crackers—it was pure heaven! I managed to make it last a whole week.

By mid-May, the war in Holland ended. The Germans retreated, and the resistance came out and took control of the streets and the government. A seemingly endless column of Canadian tanks and soldiers rolled through the streets of Rotterdam. We stood on the sidewalks cheering and waving little flags. Better days were coming!

BUDA

One day in 1943, my father came home with a puppy. It was a little ball of purple wool, and when you put it down, it ran all over. This was very exciting. I could run after it all day long, from room to room. We lived in a large, sunny apartment on the fifth floor of a twelve-story building in Rotterdam. It had a wall of glass in the front where I could climb up on the windowsill and look down on the little square below, to watch theneighborhood kids playing around on the grass-covered air raid shelter that had been built there after the German bombardment of May 1940. The sirens would still wail like wolves howling in the forest, but now the planes came from England, heading toward Germany, so we just stayed inside and waited for the "All-Clear" to sound. The bomb shelter had become a fort for us kids, and we battled around it, pushing each other down the crest.

Our square, the Ungerplein, was named after a mayor of Rotterdam. It lay along the Schiekade, the quai of the Schie Canal. I skated on the Schie in 1939 when I was four and drank hot chocolate bought from the little stand set up on stilts on the ice. But now the Schie was filled in with debris from the bombardment. An electric tram now ran along the Schiekade, and each day I would take the number two to my school, accompanied by my mother or the maid, Kati.

After school, I couldn't wait to get home to play with the new puppy. My parents decided to name it Buda, after part of the city where my mother was born, Budapest. It was a Chow, or as we said in Holland, a Chow-Chow, with dark, long hair and a purple tongue. Since I was an only child pets were my playmates. We'd had several cats—strays my mother had picked up and one my father had rescued from the plywood warehouse when his business was bombed in 1940.

The cats died or ran off, in spite of the efforts of the "cat-wife", a wizened old woman who came around to offer herbal cures and always carried a supply of fish heads wrapped in newspaper. But now I had a dog, and I could chase him up and down the long hallway where my dad and I played soccer with a tennis ball at night when he wasn't away working at his business or for the Red Cross. When I caught the puppy, I would roll him around the floor like a ball or squeeze him to hear him squeak—he was my best toy, and I was the boss of him!

I was just eight, and Buda was always going to be a puppy in my mind. But Buda grew quickly and grew tired of my rough play, so one day he wrestled free and bit me. His teeth went through the skin on my thigh, and I could see blood, so I screamed. My mother and Kati ran to take care of me, and Buda was locked in the kitchen.

From that day on there were two wars in Holland: the one outside and the one in our apartment. The war outside, I'd grown used to. It was still scary to see the German soldiers in our streets or to hear the planes flying over us at night while the sirens wailed, but I felt safe with my parents in our apartment with all the windows covered for the blackout. Now I had a new enemy—Buda, my former plaything.

In spite of our meager food rations, Buda grew quickly into a fierce beast whose teeth seemed to gnash whenever he saw me. I was so frightened that I began to scream whenever he came near me, and inevitably, he would pull his leash away from Kati to come and bite me. I wasn't the only one. He had a nasty temper and attacked people in the street whenever Kati took him for his walk. Our doorbell rang one day, and my mother opened the door to a gentleman whose sleeve had been torn from the shoulder of his jacket. Buda was an embarrassment.

For a year I tried to hide from him as best I could. I kept to my room or played on the balcony that ran along the rear of our apartment. Buda stayed in the kitchen or the foyer. Our paths seldom crossed. Friends who dared to visit us always made sure that Buda was locked away before they came in. Only my parents and Kati were safe from his wrath.

By the end of 1944, Holland had endured four years of occupation, and things were getting desperate. We had no electricity and almost no food. The only heat came from an old wood stove that had been moved into our kitchen to replace the gas range. There, my mother and Kati would boil sugar beets to make molasses and turn tulip bulbs into patties that were tasteless but edible. My father would return from his nighttime missions with black market food obtained from remote farms, and my mother kept some sausages in our pantry, which she had received from her sister in Budapest.

Outside, things were even worse. There was widespread starvation and long lines at any shop rumored to have something on its shelves—anything just to fill the stomach a bit. Almost daily, some little child from the back streets near us and dressed in rags would knock on the door to beg for food. My mother would take out a plate, and I would look at the child, close to my own age, blue with cold and covered with sores, and feel embarrassed to have roof over my head.

I was now ten years old and old enough to walk to school by myself. The school was closed for a couple of months at the end of 1944 because there was no wood to heat the classrooms, but classes resumed in early 1945. I walked home after school one day and let myself in—no one seemed to be around—so I lay down on the living room sofa and soon fell asleep. I had frequent nightmares I those days, and this time it was no different. In my dream, a dreadful weight was crushing me, and I couldn't breathe. My heart was pounding, and with a start I opened my eyes. There, two inches from my face, was Buda's head. He lay across my chest with his paws on my shoulders. I hardly dared to breathe, but nothing happened. Buda continued to stare at me dispassionately. Very slowly, limb by limb, I managed to free myself and get up. Still Buda didn't attack. I reached out to pet him, and he closed his eyes. Then I understood: as long as I didn't scream, he wouldn't bite. He even let me put a leash on his collar. I couldn't wait to take him out.

From then on, I walked Buda every day after school. I had the square mostly to myself. Neighbors who knew the dog kept their distance. I was ten years old with the world's more fearsome beast on a leash! Then one day, soon after these excursions began, I found myself surrounded by some kids from the back streets. They showed enormous interest in my dog and begged me for the leash. My chest puffed out with pride at this unexpected attention, and I gladly handed it to them.

Instantly they ran off, Buda barking in their midst, across the Schiekade and out of sight. Then a terrible realization came to me: Buda was on his way to becoming dinner! In early 1945 there were very few dogs to be seen. Most had fallen victim to the terrible hunger, which made us willing to eat whatever might stave off starvation for just another day.

I ran back to my building to get help. Two brothers, aged fifteen and seventeen, lived in the apartment above us. By a stroke of luck the younger brother was home, and he immediately ran off in the direction where Buda had vanished. Not fifteen minutes later Jan returned with Buda on his leash. He told me that he'd found Buda in the nick of time. The boys had already started the cooking fire in a nearby bombsite.

Buda lived with us through the end of the war. That summer, while we were waiting for Japan to surrender, my mother and I stayed with friends in a hotel in Warmond in the south of Holland. My father remained in Rotterdam to look after his business and to take care of Buda, who needed treatment for an infection in his left rear leg. When we returned from Warmond, Buda was gone. It turned out that one evening, as my father struggled to put medication on Buda's wound, the dog managed to wrestle free and bit him. The next day, my father told us, he took Buda back to the kennel that had bred him. We never saw him again, nor did we ever own another dog. But even today, when I see a big Chow with a purple tongue my thoughts go back to that strange and terrible year, the hunger winter of 1944.

Hans & wife Gloria. Brooklyn 1962

Hans & daughter, Melina 1995

Name: Hans Gesell

Born: Rotterdam, Holland, 1935

Paternal Grandparents
Grandfather
Louis Abrahams
B: Rotterdam, Holland, date unknown
D: date and place unknown

Maternal Grandparents
Grandfather
Emil Pataki,
B: Budapest, date unknown
D: Budapest, 1926

Grandmother
Antonia (née Gesell)
B: Wiesbaden, Germany, date unknown
D: Rotterdam, 1945

Grandmother
Gisella (née Reich)
B. Kassa, date unknown
D: Budapest, 1933

Father
Hendrik (Hans) Gesell-Abrahams
B: Rotterdam, Holland, 1894
D: Rotterdam, 1980

Mother
Lilli Livia (née Pataky)
B: Budapest, 1907
D: New York, U.S., 1990

Prewar

My mother was a musician who studied violin at the Franz Liszt Academy in Budapest, where she was a master-class student of Jenö Hubay. My father was a businessman who started his own furniture grade plywood import firm, the Holland Triplex Import. They met in Rotterdam when my mother was on tour with her all-girl orchestra, and they married in 1934.

My father's business prospered, and we lived comfortably. During the summers, my mother took me to Hungary to visit her sister Ella and my uncle Oszkar Kutasi. Ella and Oszkar also came to Rotterdam to visit us.

War

We stayed in Rotterdam right through the war. Our building was spared when half of Rotterdam went up in flames in the bombardment of May 1940

My mother's Jewish identity was concealed with false papers obtained by her sister. My father had legally changed his name to Gesell as a young man and decided to carry on as if the restriction imposed on Jews by the Germans did not apply to us. I attended kindergarten and elementary school in Rotterdam, and although the occupation caused many hardships, we made it through to the liberation in 1945.

Postwar

I attended the Erasmus Gymnasium until the summer of 1950 when my father decided to move to the United States, fearing the Soviet threat in Europe. We arrived in September 1950 and moved in with cousins in Montclair, New Jersey.

My mother planned to resume her musical career with ex-colleagues from the Liszt academy, but she was diagnosed with multiple sclerosis, which ended her career.

I graduated high school in 1952 and then went on to college, first to Kenyon in Ohio, then to City College in New York. In 1958, I received my bachelor's degree in civil engineering and went to work for firms specializing in working with architects on a great variety of buildings.

In CCNY, I met my wife-to-be, Gloria, who graduated with a degree in psychology. We were married in 1964 and have one child, a daughter, Melina, who is now a lawyer for the administration of Children's Services in New York. Gloria is a consultant for Head Start programs in the Bronx, and I still work for the same engineering firm that I joined in 1962.

We love to travel and frequently visit both Holland and Hungary to stay connected to our roots.

Budapest 1941

Erika Hecht

CONVERSION

"You have to behave," my mother said. "You have to be very, very good."

Her voice was serious, low, and threatening, and her grip on my hand was firm as she pulled me along with her. We were walking toward a big yellow building.

"This is a church," she said.

"Watch your step," she said.

And, "What are you staring at?" as I stumbled on the steps leading to the entrance of the church. I was still looking up to see how tall the church was. Mother picked me up impatiently and carried me the rest of the way to the entrance. Somehow, I knew and understood that she was afraid. I was three and a half years old.

We went inside. It was dark and smelled of burning wood like our stove at home when the fire was about to go out. Many candles were burning near the walls, but it was still too dark to make out the pictures above them. I was cold and frightened and told my mother that I wanted to leave.

"No," she said, "NO, no, no!" I started to cry, but to no avail. She continued to pull me along with her, toward the front. "The *Pater* is waiting for us," she said. "Now stop crying, don't ask questions, and be a good little girl."

"Where are the birds?" I asked next, as we passed the birdbath on the way to the front. It looked exactly like the one in my cousin Marika's garden. Mother stopped for a moment, and then she said, "That is holy water. Now you must really be quiet or else!"

The *Pater* wore a long black dress. He stood on the stairs in front of a railing. I could see two boys standing behind him and wondered why they were wearing nightshirts. The *Pater* started to speak to my mother slowly in a low voice. He was very serious. I could not understand anything he was saying. Mother was listening, nodding, and even talking to the *Pater* without paying any attention to me. I was getting bored. I said I wanted to go home. I said that I was hungry, but she continued to listen only to the priest. Suddenly, my mother knelt down on the step in front of the priest. Why was she doing that? Was there some dirt on the floor that she wanted to clean? Did she see a bug? No, she was still looking up at the priest, listening. I was so frightened I started to cry again. When the priest put something in my mother's mouth, my crying turned into a wail, and I wailed and cried and continued to cry even as we were leaving the church.

Outside, the sun was shining. It was warm, so why was my mother shivering? Two ladies, her friends, were waiting for us. They were speaking to her, comforting her, and telling her that everything was going to be all right. They told me to be a good girl, to stop crying, stop sobbing. But I could not. Mother lifted me up, and I saw that she too was crying. She continued to carry me as we were walking away from the church, bouncing me up and down to comfort me or maybe herself. She kept repeating the same words louder and louder: "We are Christians now. We are Catholics. We are safe. The bastards cannot hurt us. Nobody can hurt us. We are Christians."

Montreal 1960

Sag Harbor NY 2006, with grandchildren Sam and Oli

Name: Erika Hecht (née Erika Hiekisch)

Born: Budapest, 1934

Paternal Grandparents	**Maternal Grandparents**
Grandfather	**Grandfather**
Richard Hiekisch	Béla Ács
B: Place and date unknown	**B:** Place and date unknown
D: Budapest, date unknown	**D:** Budapest ghetto, 1945
Grandmother	**Grandmother**
Katalin Bleier (née Szusz)	Adel (née Schwartz)
B: Place and date unknown	**B:** Esztergom, Hungary,
D: Sydney, Australia, 1975	**D:** Budapest, 1947
Father	**Mother**
Henry (Bleier) Hiekisch	Georgina (née Ács)
B: Budapest, 1906	**B:** Budapest, 1909
D: Sydney, 1992	**D:** Vienna, Austria, 1996

Prewar

The family that I was born into was middle-class on my mother's side and artistic and bohemian on my father's. My circumstances, at a very early age, were influenced by increasing anti-Semitism and the accompanying restrictions on Jewish life. My mother, already divorced from my half-Jewish father, converted to Catholicism to possibly help us save our lives, and she sent me to Christian schools.

War

In the spring of 1944, my mother, myself, and my half-sister went into hiding in a small village in western Hungary. We had false papers that gave us different names and identities. The area where we were hiding eventually became a fierce battleground between the retreating German army and the advancing Soviets. Our village was occupied and reoccupied by the Russians several times. We had to flee ahead of the Germans in January 1945 after it was discovered that we were Jews. Between December 1944 and March 1945, we hid in empty bombed-out houses, ditches, and abandoned barns. We no longer had documents, food, or money and survived by stealing, begging, and by the mercy of some decent strangers. In the last weeks before liberation, we survived the fierce bombings and the last round-up of Jews by the retreating Germans, hiding in caves in the mountains on the northern shore of the Balaton (a large lake in Hungary)

Postwar

Back in Budapest in June of 1945, we discovered that only a few of our relatives had survived. Nevertheless, life slowly returned to "normal." I was sent back to school and continued to attend Catholic religious classes. In 1948, the family decided to leave Hungary ahead of the Communist takeover of the government and flee to Vienna before the Iron Curtain descended. We were refugees again.

My education continued, first in Vienna then in London. After receiving my British school-leaving certificate, I returned to Vienna and attended medical school. During my internship at a Vienna hospital, I met my future husband, a Hungarian/Czech Jew, already established in Montreal, Canada. We got married and I moved to Montreal. There was no reciprocity between the Austrian and Canadian Universities and I was prevented from practicing medicine unless I returned to school for two years. I chose to stay home for a number of years and raise three children, take care of the extended family and support my husband's growing interest and role in the Jewish community.

Architecture and design had always been of great interest to me. After my children entered school, I started a decorating business and soon became quite successful and well-known.

Life to the Present

I divorced my husband in 1987 and continued to live in Montreal for a while. In 1991, I participated in the first Hidden Child Conference held in New York City. It was a memorable experience. It finally clarified and confirmed my Jewish identity. My involvement in the group continues and remains a very important and satisfactory part of my life. I moved to New York City in 1997, where I continue to participate in many activities of Hidden Children groups.

Kapuvár, Susan age 3

Susan Kalev

ROOTED IN THE PAST

My mother used to recall with a sense of pride that people told her she was foolish to be pregnant in 1944. She held on to some irrational sense of faith. She was able to survive— pregnant and with a three-year-old—in a Budapest ghetto for months because a relative chose to include her on a special family Zionist list. Instead of being shipped off to Auschwitz from Pápa she was transported to a Budapest internment camp and then to a ghetto. My uncle was the *Rosh Hakal* of the Pápa synagogue and was permitted to save his own family.

In the summer of 1944, I was born in the Budapest internment camp, and now my mother had two little girls to care for. While she worked inside, I slept in a basket on the ground of the inner courtyard. When I was one week old, a German officer standing on the balcony above flipped his cigarette butt into the yard, and I caught on fire. The flames quickly engulfed my pillow, and my screams brought my mother running to the courtyard. The shock of seeing me on fire immediately stopped the flow of her milk. I was rushed back to the hospital where I was born, with third degree burns. There was nothing they could do for me— they smeared me with Vaseline and my mother was told to wait out the first critical twenty-four hours. She gave me transfusions of blood and spent her nights waking up every few hours to rotate my head from side to side so the damaged skin on my neck would not harden into scar tissue. I survived the burn, and because she could no longer nurse me, she would chew on beans and peas and put the softly chewed food into my mouth. That first year I developed a huge pot belly with stick-thin arms and legs and a scar down my neck and shoulder. But I was strong; my older sister Mari succumbed to a childhood disease and died.

So it was that my mother and I alone remained, and in January 1945, when the Russians entered Budapest, she was left to fend for herself and for her infant. She walked the streets of Budapest hungry and cold, all of twenty-seven years old, not knowing if any of her family would be coming home. She made her way back to Pápa, my father's hometown, and lived in the house where she had spent her marriage. She would find out soon that no one would be coming back—not my father, not her sister, not her parents.

Later that year, my mother was sitting on the balcony of her Pápa house when a man from nearby Kapuvár walked by. He was an older man she and her family had known since her childhood. He was on his way to a Jewish wedding. They had not met in many years. It turned out that he had lost his wife and children to the war and was alone. He and my mother got to

153

talking, and he never made it to the wedding. The following year they married, and thus my earliest memories are from our big house in Kapuvár. Two years later, a younger sister, Marika, was born. In the small town of Kapuvár I was the sole surviving Jewish child of school age. I recall rushing home from the one-room school one day and asking our nanny what the word "Jew" meant.

Until I was ten years old, I believed that my stepfather was my biological parent; my parents almost never spoke of the war years or of the families they had lost. After I found out, I insisted on staying inside for the synagogue services when they recited the Kaddish, or the prayer for the dead.

I knew my mother only as a Holocaust survivor, but from glimpses over the years and from the tales of other cousins, I began to slowly understand the enormity of the losses in her life—from a traditional Orthodox Jewish family, with sheltering and loving parents and a talented sister, a family life rooted in stability, order, and comfort, she was suddenly thrust into the world. She, who was taught to cook and bake and sew and keep a kosher home, to speak French and German, who was comforted by the predictability of her very existence, now had to give blood for transfusions and chewed peas for her starving infant. She now was alone in an insane and terrifying world. She once told me that she had returned to Sopron, her hometown, to search for some silverware that had been left for safekeeping with Gentile neighbors. She heard the grumblings of others in the town, "Those Jews, you can't get rid of them – more came back after Hitler than lived here before Hitler."

My father had been sent to a German labor camp, and in uncharacteristic fashion, my mother confided to me that he returned home only once to see her. During that one night, she became pregnant with me. I have often imagined that one night of love when I began, and I have often visualized what my father would be like, how he would look down on me from heaven and be proud of me. In my regular trips back to Hungary, I visit the homes of my parents and the grandparents I never knew and envision my life there with them. I walk the streets my mother grew up on – I touch the orderly red brick stones of her school building and breathe the same air into my lungs. I gaze at the women in town my own age now and think that could be me. This is what my life would have been. I sometimes want the life that was taken away from me. I want not only to survive my history, but to live my history. I want to return to mother.

My mother never wanted to return to Hungary after we escaped in the 1956 Revolution. Ten years of my talking finally opened something in her, and she thought she could take on the memories. In 1992, after thirty-six years, I took her back with me. In her parents' home in Sopron, she stood in the garden her father had built and silent tears tore from her. The woman who now lived there, a simple peasant who remembered my parents and saw me as an infant, stood nearby and understood. I have always been the repository of my mother's past, the living reminder and remainder of her first life — since her death ten years ago, I carry on the legacy of her life. I feel somehow more connected to the past than to my present life. My real self is still anchored back in Budapest. And it keeps my mother alive within me.

Kapuvár 1948, Susan, center, age 4

New York, with daughters, Nehara (L) and Edya (R)

New York 2007

Name: Susan Kalev (Née Zsuzsa Weltner, Steiner when mother remarried)

Born: July 1944, Budapest

Paternal Grandparents	**Maternal Grandparents**
Grandfather	**Grandfather**
Mano Weltner:	Henri Spiegel
B. Pápa, date unknown	**B**: date and place unknown
D: Pápa, 1938	**D**: Beaten to death in the ghetto,1944
Grandmother	**Grandmother**
Matilda (Née Züsz)	Franci (Née Weisz)
B: date and Place unknown	**B**: Dunaszerdahely, year unknown
D: Budapest, 1944	**D**: 1944, place unknown
Father	**Mother**
Henrik Weltner	Ilona (Née Spiegel)
B: Pápa , 1911	**B**: Kapuvár, 1917
B: German labor camp, 1944	**D**: New York City, 1996

Prewar and War

The family was Orthodox, and my mother had a traditional well-to-do Jewish upbringing. She grew up in Sopron and was able to escape deportation to Auschwitz while pregnant with me because she was put on a special list by a relative. My older sister, age three, died, and none of my immediate family survived. My father was sent to labor camp in Germany and did not return.

Postwar

My mother remarried two years after the war and moved to Kapuvár, where I and later another sister named Marika lived with our parents until 1951, when the Russians came and took everything away. We moved to Budapest, and I attended regular school until grade seven. Three weeks after the 1956 Revolution broke out, we escaped on foot to Austria. We stayed in lagers and refugee camps until we arrived in New York City in December 1956. I was twelve.

My mother worked as a seamstress in Budapest and later in New York. She studied and was employed as a bookkeeper for twenty-five years.

Life to the Present

At age twenty, while a student at Hunter College, I visited Israel and fell in love with the country and the man I soon married. I continued my studies at the Hebrew University and got my degree in social work. After five years, my daughter Edya was born in Israel. Later, we moved back to New York, where our second daughter, Nehara, was born. Edya is now a museum educator and yoga instructor. Nehara and her husband are both dancers and choreographers in Los Angeles.

I work as a social worker consultant within the Jewish community and enjoy traveling. I am happy that my life included living in three different cultures and speaking three languages. I became a vegetarian and speak out for animal rights out of compassion for their suffering.

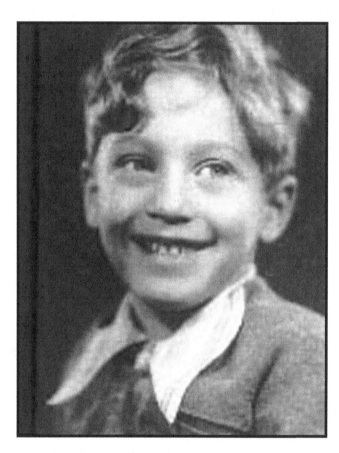

Budapest 1937

Peter Klepa

CLOSE CALLS

Survival of Jewish children during the Holocaust was precarious, often miraculous, and rare, as the final numbers demonstrate. The survivors were left with a sense of bewilderment and awe, wondering, often for the rest of their lives, what the difference was between sheer luck, fate or coincidence.

My own experiences are almost too incredulous, for it happened not once, not twice nor three times, but four times (and once shortly after liberation) that my life was snatched from the jaws of death and that I am here to tell the tale.

1.

On a moonless night in September 1942, we were asleep, when around 2 A.M., in the quiet of the night, we were jolted out of bed by a horrendous, shattering explosion.

My mother, stepfather, and I lived near the top of Rozsadomb (Rose Hill) on the Buda side of the city, a quiet residential area of villas and a few smaller apartment houses. Some windows broke, but owing to the blackout, we couldn't see anything. Badly shaken, we eventually all went back to sleep.

The next morning I went exploring and found, through a fluke, that the first-ever Russian bomb to reach Budapest had squarely hit the villa next door, which belonged to a famous Hungarian author/playwright named Leslie Zilahy. He and his wife had been spared. They were attending a late dinner party across the Danube. However, their two children and their nanny had been killed instantly.

That huge bomb exploded less than one hundred yards from my bedroom!

2.

Later, in early 1944, Budapest came under the first of many "formal" air attacks by the Allied powers, complete with air raid warnings on the radio and sirens. This was new to us, and the first night we took blankets and sat on a nearby hillside, with a full view of the city, to watch the most spectacular sight I had ever seen in my life: the droning bombers overhead, the long line of curving, glowing tracers of red-ack-ack antiaircraft fire, the bright searchlights stabbing the sky seeking planes to put into their cross hairs, and the overwhelming noise of the explosions. It was truly awesome to see!

The next morning we went back to the hillside where we had watched that incredible show and found the place where we had been sitting. The entire area was saturated with spent and jagged pieces of shrapnel.

In our innocence we had not realized that all that shrapnel could have easily cut us to ribbons. Once again, fate had intervened.

3.

When the Germans entered Hungary on March 19, 1944, we initially hid in the apartments of friends and made several hasty and clandestine moves into different "Jewish Star" houses and managed to live through that difficult summer and early fall. By the time the Arrow Cross fascists took over in mid-October, with the Soviet army already approaching Budapest, my mother and I were on the run again, ending up in yet another "Jewish House" on the Buda side of the Margaret Bridge. On the second night, a group of black-clad Nazi SS officers walked through the building. Unbeknownst to us, they were Adolf Eichman's men "taking inventory" of the Jews in the building. My mother must have had a premonition, because the minute the Nazis left, she grabbed our suitcase and we left. Fortunately, there were no guards in the building. We went up into the Buda hills, where she left me in the care of a Catholic orphanage while she went into hiding with Christian friends. It was only after the war that we learned that all the Jewish residents in that apartment building had been had been taken to the Danube and murdered the following day!

4.

In early December, my grandfather took me from the Catholic orphanage back to the Pest side, where we joined my grandmother in a Raoul Wallenberg "protected house" in the "International Ghetto". By that time, we all had the Swedish Embassy–issued life-saving *Schutzpass* document.

It was cold and windy as we walked across the Chain Bridge, and in the twilight I saw my first dead body lying in the street. The Soviet army had the city nearly surrounded by then, and all public services were breaking down. At first we still had sporadic electricity and water service, but all that ceased around mid-December. With all our windows blown out by the bombardment and concussions, we lived in our coats and sweaters and had only some dried peas and beans to eat. Water came from a single trickling spigot in the courtyard or melted snow. Instead of fighting or escaping, the Hungarian Arrow Cross thugs were still robbing and killing defenseless Jews.

Some strange noises coming from across the street woke me up around 3 A.M., a day in late December. I peered out cautiously and saw that the Yellow Star apartment house across the street was being emptied of all its Jewish tenants. Young Arrow Cross thugs and other teenaged boys armed with German submachine guns were lining up the Jews and marching them toward the Danube.

It was only a few years ago, while reading a book about Raoul Wallenberg's activities in 1944 Budapest, that I chanced upon a chapter relating to this incident.

Apparently Wallenberg had been frantically notified that an atrocity was about to take place, but it took an extra thirty minutes for the Swedish embassy car to get through the rubble blocking the streets, and by the time he arrived, there was no one left except a few Arrow Cross men looting empty apartments. Meanwhile, all the Jews had been lined up at the edge of the Danube, tied together in threes, and with one bullet fired into the middle person, shoved into the icy waters to drown. By that time, even the Arrow Cross had to save their bullets.

When Wallenberg asked one of the fascist thugs at the scene, "Why are you men doing this?" The man answered, "Why not? They are only dirty Jews!"

I will never know why the Arrow Cross selected that particular building and not ours, just across the street, but blind luck saved my life once again.

5. (After liberation)

After the siege finally ended in February 1945 with the Germans and their Arrow Cross cohorts beaten and on the run, my mother decided that the best place for me was out of Budapest, where the Soviet army was looting, raping, and killing. I was to go to the large ex-manor house of a nobleman in Fót, northeast of the capital, where the Catholic Church was now running an orphanage. Numerous deep trenches, some fifteen-foot deep, had been dug across the two-lanes in a futile attempt to stop the Soviet tanks. The horse-drawn wagons, which were the only transports available to civilian, had to carefully maneuver around them. A Russian army truck full of soldiers was impatient to pass our slow-moving caravan. As the driver shouldered past us, his fender caught the corner of our wagon and pushed it forward, toward the horses that were pulling it as well as toward the deep tank-trap. The horses panicked, and our open wagon was about to flip over when the driver managed to disengage and pull past us, laughing uproariously. Shaken, but safe once again, we continued our journey and I spent three safe months in Fót.

In the fall of 1945, I went back to Budapest and resumed my schooling.

Los Angeles 1952

Los Angeles 2006

Los Angeles 2008, Susan Klepa, daughter Lilian, son Robert and Peter

Name: Peter P. Klepa

Born: Budapest, Hungary, 1933

Paternal Grandparents	**Maternal Grandparents**
Grandfather	**Grandfather**
Anton Kleinberger	Béla Weisz
B: Place unknown, 1879	**B:** Place unknown, 1885
D: Los Angeles, United States, 1957	**D:** London, England, 1974
Grandmother	**Grandmother**
Malvin (née Horovitz)	Olga (née Fleischmann)
B: Budapest, Hungary, 1882	**B:** Budapest, Hungary, 1888
D: Los Angeles, United States, 1952	**D:** London, England, 1976
Father	**Mother**
Paul Kleinberger (Klepa)	Irene (née Weisz)
B: Budapest, Hungary, 1907	**B:** Budapest, Hungary, 1909
D: Los Angeles, United States, 1964	**D:** London, England, 1979

Prewar

I was born into two affluent Jewish merchant families. I was an only child. My parents divorced when I was two and a half years old, and in 1937, my grandmother made the entire maternal side of the family convert to Roman Catholicism. Although in school I was taught as a Catholic, in the end, all my Catholic papers and schooling meant nothing because to the Nazis, all Jews were just Jews …

After divorcing my mother in 1938, my father moved to Paris and worked in the French movie industry.

War

My father escaped the invading Nazi armies in 1940 and made his way to America. In the meantime, my mother married a half-Jewish vice president of BAUXIT, (the aluminum exporting company of Hungary). After the German invasion, the (Hungarian) Nazi laws forced us to move into a yellow-star designated villa with many other Jewish families, and our Holocaust odyssey began.

My grandparents obtained life-saving *Schutzpass* documents from Raoul Wallenberg. After the Arrow-Cross took over the government, even more oppressive times began for the Jews.

In the evening hours, when the general noise of the city subsided, we could hear the murmur of the Soviet/Russian artillery approaching from the East. During the siege, we were bombed, rocketed, mortared, starved, and hunted by the Arrow Cross. It was the first time I had known sustained hunger.

After the siege of Budapest, we were liberated by Soviet (Mongol) troops of the Russian army in mid-January, 1945.

Fortunately one way or another, everyone in my immediate family survived the war!

Postwar

In the fall of 1945, I resumed Gymnasium studies and also attended a special design/graphics school to polish my artistic talents. My father helped with financial arrangements from Los Angeles. He had married an American woman while serving in the U.S. Army, and ironically, he ran a Nazi prisoner-of-war camp in Louisiana. In June 1948, at fifteen years of age, I left Hungary alone, on my way to America. My mother was trapped behind the Iron Curtain and was unable to leave Hungary. Sadly, I never saw her again …

In Los Angeles, I studied remedial English and spoke it fluently by the time I finished junior high school in 1949, the year I became an American citizen. Three years of high school followed, and after graduation came two and a half years of Community College.

The compulsory military draft caught up with me in 1954, and I spent two years in the U.S. Army Signal Corps, including fourteen months in Japan as part of the American occupation forces. I was so glad to be an American that I considered it an honor to serve. The G.I. Bill paid for my college education, and I subsequently earned my Industrial Design degree from the prestigious Art Center College of Design in Los Angeles.

Life to the Present

During my second year of working as an apprentice industrial designer, through a fortunate blind date, I met wonderful Susan Richter, who was also a Hungarian child survivor of the Holocaust from Budapest. We were married in February 1960. We had three children: Vivian, Lilian and Robert. We lost Vivian in a tragic accident when she was just two years old. Over time, I worked up the professional advancement ladder to become Account Manager at a design firm, then Director of Design for a company allied with upcoming computer/aerospace corporations. In late 1969, I opened my own design firm, which I ran successfully for twenty-five years. Our two children were healthy, smart, and good students. Daughter Lilian obtained a master's degree in psychology and an MBA, finishing at Claremont College with a PhD in psychology. She now lives in New Jersey with her family and has three wonderful children. (About eleven years ago, much to our surprise, she turned to Orthodoxy in her religious beliefs and found a fine husband with similar interests.) Our son, Robert, attended Loyola Law School and became an attorney. He lives in Los Angeles with his wife.

I retired in 1994 and have since written several books (a "How-to-Travel book and a collection of episodes from my life and Holocaust experiences titled *Facets of my Life*). Recently, I printed and donated four copies of it to Chapman University's Holocaust Library.

I am now involved in a long-term project, writing and illustrating my family's history for future generations. The completed seven books blend political, world history, and important technical and scientific occurrences with family photos and nostalgia from the late-1800s to 1975. I am currently working on book number eight, bringing the narrative up to 1980.

I have served on the Board of Directors of the Child Survivors of the Holocaust, Los Angeles, and made many friends there. Susan and I still enjoy the group's many activities, and I still help the group whenever I can, for example, as in their own new autobiography project. Over the years, Susan and I traveled around the world visiting, over sixty countries and all seven continents. Whenever school vacations allowed, we took our children along with us.

Nowadays, we most often fly to New Jersey to visit our three grandchildren, sometimes combining the visits with trips to other destinations. We also pursue a very active social and cultural life.

We recently celebrated our happy forty-seventh (!) wedding anniversary.

America has been wonderful to me and my family. It gave us opportunities I could not have had anywhere else, and it has my grateful, lifelong appreciation.

1943 with father in Budapest

Marielle Lang

RECOVERED MEMORIES

I only remember one event from my past as a "Hidden Child". I was five years old in October 1944 when it happened. At that time I wasn't yet hidden in the sense of having to take on a different identity or remain in a secret place for a long time. That came later. The memory is powerful enough to have stayed with me, while I have lost all other recollections of war, bombardment, and hiding. Still, what I have forgotten and what I remember have been playing a game of hide-and-seek in my mind, as over the years I have been trying to discover what really took place on a particular evening in Budapest in the fall of 1944. I have found at least three versions of this experience: mine, my mother's and my cousin, Juli's. The place and the characters vary, but they all have in common one incident, which I believe lies at the root of a strange phobia I have had all my life.

My Story

My grandparents lived at Legrády Károly utca 39. In October 1944, I was there with my grandparents and my mother. One night, there was the sound of loud knocking at the door: an ominous sound in the middle of the night. Some men entered.

After we let them in, these men told us to get dressed because they were going to take us "somewhere". I didn't know where, just that we had to put on our clothes in order to leave our apartment in the middle of the night and it was cold outside. Someone helped me into my clothes and buttoned my coat. Everyone seemed ready to go, when suddenly our visitors changed their minds.

"We have enough people," they said. "Wait for us. We will be back to get you later." Then they left, and we hid in the bathroom. We probably stayed in our hiding place all night, and then the next day we went somewhere else.

To this memory, my adult self added the words, "We have enough Jews to shoot into the Danube tonight."

My Mother's Story

Some men from the Arrow Cross came to pick us up in the middle of the night in October, 1944. The janitor hid us in the garage. That's how we escaped.

My mother's way of dealing with memories of the war is to simply wipe the slate clean. She doesn't want to talk about what happened then. It's hard for me to get answers to any of my questions. She claims that she doesn't remember because she is too old, but I know that even when she was younger, she never wanted to discuss the subject.

I suppose that's why my memories have faded. In other families, stories, shared and repeated, keep the recollections of child survivors alive. The various versions of events as told by different witnesses mesh to become the accepted form of the event. In my family, nobody talked about what we experienced during 1944–45. There were no stories to share.

The only member of my family willing to talk about the war was my cousin, Juli, who lives in Amsterdam. For some reason, we weren't in touch with each other for years. When we finally met fifteen years ago, she told me that she had written a book about her wartime experiences. Three years older than me, she is my best source for filling in the blanks about the fateful night.

Juli's Story

My parents and I lived with our grandparents in their apartment, just like you and your mother. In Budapest at that time Jews were permitted to live only in the so-called "starred (Jewish) houses". That's why many families were obliged to crowd together.

One night in October 1944, some men burst into the apartment. They were Nyilas, the Hungarian Arrow Cross. They told my father to get dressed and follow them. The reason they gave was that he would be sent to do munkaszolgálat, to join a forced labor unit made up of Jewish men. My father obediently put on his clothes and did as he was told. He never returned.

As soon as the men left the house, the janitor's wife, who was not Jewish, hurried us out of the apartment and led us into the laundry room in the attic (the space where wet laundry was hung on lines stretched from wall to wall) so we could hide in case the Nyilas came back for us. That's how we were saved.

To her story, Juli added:

To this day, I can't forgive myself for something horrible I did that night. I actually helped my father put on his socks. I keep reproaching myself, imagining that if I hadn't done that, he wouldn't have been ready to leave in time. Would he have been saved then?

Talking to Juli helped me finally to understand the strange phobia I have had all my life: a horror of going into a bathroom with a *fregoli*, a wooden frame suspended from the ceiling across which lines of thin cord are strung to hang wet laundry washed by hand. When in use, this contraption can be lowered to eye level.

Whether we hid from the Arrow Cross that night in a bathroom, as I imagined, or the laundry room in the attic, according to Juli's account, doesn't seem to matter anymore. What is real is the feeling in the pit of my stomach, the memory of the fear I had experienced when I was five years old, crouching in my winter coat hiding behind lines of wet laundry all night.

Morocco 1962

On the occasion of Mother's 90th Birthday in Frankfort, Germany
From left: Marielle, daughter Anita, Granddaughters,
Elena, Benedicte & Emma, daughter Alexandra
Front: Grandson, Eliott, Mother, grandson, Spencer

Name: Marielle Lang (née Lipscher, changed to Lippai)

Born: 1939, Bournemouth, England

Paternal Grandparents	Maternal Grandparents
Grandfather	**Grandfather**
Dr. Sándor Lipscher	Dr. Béla Hodos (Haberfeld)
B: Unknown	**B**: Dombovár 1878.
D: Budapest 1951	**D**: Frankfurt, Germany, 1966
Grandmother	**Grandmother**
Ethel (Née Reichenberger)	Margit (née Fodor)
B. Place unknown, 1873	**B**: Budapest,1892
D: 1961, Cuba	**D**: Frankfurt, Germany, 1988
Father	**Mother**
Steve Lipscher (Lippai)	Ibolya (née Hodos)
B: Budapest, 1906	**B**. Budapest, 1918
D: Paris, France, 1971	

War

I was born in England because my father was employed there by the GUMMI GYÁR (*Magyar Rugganyárugyár*) rubber factory, a Hungarian rubber manufacturing company. In 1940, we went back to Hungary because my mother insisted that she couldn't leave her parents alone.

My father was called up for forced labor—*munkaszolgálat*—and my aunt arranged for me to be taken in by nuns. I remember spending time with my aunt, but only one episode with my mother. My only recollection of liberation is of Soviet soldiers coming into the cellar where we were hiding and giving me a piece of bread.

Postwar

My parents divorced immediately after the war and my mother remarried in 1946. In 1949, I, my mother, and my step-father, with expensively purchased exit visas, left Hungary for Paris. Shortly after, we went to England, where I was placed in a boarding school. Later, we went back to Paris and from there to Frankfurt, Mainz, and Baden Baden, Germany, where I attended French schools. After high school, I studied at the Sprachen und Dolmetscher Institut (an interpreter's school) in Munich.

In 1960, I came to the United States and worked for Swissair and met my future husband, Dr. János (Jean) Lang, an ob-gyn.

Life to the Present

After marriage, we moved to Rabat, Morocco, where we lived for seven years, but going to Paris to give birth to my two daughters. When my husband was promised an equivalency of his medical degree, we moved to Paris (his degree was from Germany.) The equivalency degree did not materialize, and after a two-year struggle, we moved to Frankfurt, where he opened a very successful private practice. We lived there until 1978. When the European Union came into being, my husband's medical degree became valid in France. We moved to Cannes, France.

I divorced in 1987 and moved to the United States, where both my daughters were in college. I have lived in New York ever since.

I travel a great deal, visiting family. I love the theater, books, walking, and most of all, my five grandchildren.

Budapest 1944

Ildi Marshall

MY TWO WARS

I remember things, but not full stories with beginnings, middle, or ends. During the whole time of Nazi occupation and the reign of terror of the *Nyilas* (Arrow Cross), my major anxiety was not the war that was tearing the world apart, but the private war going on in my family. My parents were always fighting, and divorce was a constant threat. While families were desperate to stay together and were scrambling to find hiding places that allowed them to do so, my mother and I were always taking shelter in a different cellar than my father during the bombing raids. We were never together.

I do remember one time when we were huddling in the cellar and a group of Arrow Cross thugs came in, looking for workers for forced labor. They took any able-bodied people, men or women, but left behind those who had children: if they caught Jews in their net, so much the better. There was a Jewish couple in the cellar, and they didn't have a child. I remember the look of desperation on their faces as the Arrow Cross moved down the line.

There was a Christian family with six children down there with us. The Jewish lady slipped out of the line toward the Christian mother and, whispering, pleaded with her to let her borrow one of the children and say that it was her own. The Christian mother was terrified, too, probably fearing that if the Jews were caught, they might take her child along too. The whispering became more and more urgent as the Arrow Cross came closer to our corner. I could see the mother looking from one of her children to the other, wondering whether she would be sacrificing a son or a daughter by letting the Jewish woman borrow one of them. Then suddenly, as the Fascists came toward our dark corner, the mother pushed a child into the arms of the Jewish lady, who put her arms around him and stood back in line. The Fascists passed on.

One day, my mother disappeared for what seemed a very long time, and I went to live with our neighbor. Then, she reappeared looking sick and bedraggled, and I was frightened and didn't want to go back to her and cried. The neighbor sat her down, and over a cup of wartime chicory coffee, my mother tearfully told her the story of where she had been while I eavesdropped, the adults never thinking the story would interest a child.

It seems that my mother was arrested and detained along with hundreds of other Jews and eventually, when enough had been arrested, the long column of detainees was forced to march east. She had no idea where they were going. After several hours, as one of the guards was plodding next to her, my mother asked him, "What would happen if I just left the column?"

He glared at her and answered, "I'm going to pretend I didn't hear what you said," and she saw him tighten the grip on his rifle.

The following day, however, my mother managed to slip out of the column, and when it had passed, started retracing her steps. After several hours of walking, she took a rest and sat down by the roadside. Before she could hide, a German patrol car drove by and stopped. The two soldiers got out and asked her what she was doing there alone. She burst into tears and told them she was trying to get back to Budapest where she had a six-year-old child who was alone. They told her to get into the car. The car turned around and sped back toward Budapest. They drove her right to our front door. When they let her out, one of them said, "We are very sorry, Madam, but there is a war going on. However, not all Germans are alike. We wish you luck." And they sped away.

The siege of Budapest followed. Then the war in Europe was finally over a few months later, but the war in my family continued. Instead of being grateful we had all lived through that barbaric insanity, my parents continued their feud for a few more years. It was an on-again/off-again relationship that finally ended in divorce, shortly after which my father died. The horror of the war, the huddling in cellars, the fear of the bombs, the worry over food and the constant dread of betrayal are all enmeshed in my memory with the unremitting bitterness and upheavals in my own unhappy family. Sometimes I wish that it were only the war I remembered.

Budapest 1952

New York 2006

Name: Ildiko Marshall (née Ildiko Hlavathy)

Born: Budapest, 1937

Paternal Grandparents	Maternal Grandparents:
	Grandfather
Unknown	Árpad Nádor
	B: Kaposvár, date unknown
	D: Budapest, 1941
"	**Grandmother**
	Karolina (née Nattan)
	B: Kaposvár, date unknown
	D: Budapest, 1967
Father	**Mother**
András Hlavathy	Zsofia (née Nádor)
B: Sárospatak, 1897	**B:** Budapest,1908
D: Budapest, 1951	**D:** Budapest,1977

Prewar

I was born into a well-off, middle class family. My parents were business people, and I was taken care of by nannies. My father was a well-known hair stylist to movie and stage stars. My mother owned a fine lingerie boutique, to which the merchandise was supplied by my grandmother's small factory. My parents were constantly "at war," and their marriage finally ended in divorce.

War

During the war, my mother and I hid in the cellar of house building on the Madács Tér. At one point, she was taken away and marked for deportation, but she was able to escape from the column and came home. During her absence, I was taken care of by the superintendent of our building and then by my father. My parents were themselves warring at that time, so we were not together. Though they both escaped deportation, my mother's two brothers, Daniel and Laszlo Nador, both perished: the former in a Russian prison camp, the latter in Auschwitz.

Postwar

I attended several schools owing to my parents divorce in 1945 and to the moves that followed that sad happening. My father died in 1951. The schools included the Evangelikus, Notre Dame De Sion, and Dohány utca. I was eventually enrolled in the Magyar Optikai Muvek (optical training school), where I got my diploma as a technical optician. At night I studied fashion sketching.

Life to the Present

During the 1956 Revolution, I escaped Hungary with my fiancé. We came to America and were the first refugee couple to be married in Camp Kilmer. I continued working as a technical optician, but I studied fashion design until I broke into the field in the early sixties. I worked as a designer in New York's Garment Industry for twenty years before opening my own business in 1982. Meanwhile, I divorced in 1962 and remarried an American, Malcolm Marshall, in 1967. Seven years later, we were also divorced.

I continue working at my business.

I love dancing, art, music, movies, and being with my friends, the other Hungarian Hidden Children.

Zilah, Transylvania 1942

Tutzi Marton

A CHILDHOOD IN FLIGHT

In 1940, when I was three and a half and my brother was seven and a half, we took a sudden car trip from Bucharest, where I was born, to Transylvania, where my parents hailed from and where most of our extended family still lived. I didn't know until recently that we took that trip because my father's loyal chauffeur, Mr. Suciu, had warned him that the Iron Guard was about to arrest him and his whole family and probably kill us all. Mr. Suciu was arrested, tortured, and killed, but he never revealed where we had fled.

At that time, Transylvania ("Erdély" in Hungarian) was part of Romania. Though it was already under the thumb of the fascist Iron Guard, the atrocities they were committing against the Jews in Bucharest were not yet practiced in Transylvania.

Before we left, my maternal grandfather, a well-known architect who was a Polish national, had asked my mother to procure forged documents for him, stating he was a Christian. He was concerned about his citizenship status. My mother then decided to get false documents for all of us.

We arrived in Transylvania and visited several towns where relatives lived. We were staying with an aunt in Kolozsvár (Cluj) the day Admiral Horthy, with Hitler's blessing, annexed part of Transylvania, which had a predominantly Hungarian population. Horthy, regent of Hungary, marched into Kolozsvár, the major city of the region, and there, he declared the area united with Hungary.

We were now cut off from the rest of Romania.

We moved to the town of Zilah, at the foot of the Carpathian Mountains, where my mother registered herself, my brother, and me using the false Christian documents she had provided for us before leaving Bucharest. She couldn't do as much for my father because he was well known in the place, having grown up there. He was an enterprising businessman and, in spite of this setback, managed to establish a prosperous transportation business.

Shortly after our arrival in Zilah, Jewish refugees started to arrive from German-occupied Poland. They were hunted, frightened people who tried to tell everyone of the terrible atrocities being committed against the Jews. But the Hungarian Jews didn't believe them, calling the newcomers liars and refusing them any help. By then, my grandfather and grandmother had managed to join us. Since my grandfather spoke Polish, he took these rumors seriously. Besides, he had more foresight and recognized the signs of the danger looming for the Jews of Transylvania.

I was too young to fully understand everything, but in retrospect I realize that grandfather had extensive underground connections, and both my brother and I were drawn into the web of the resistance. I was very little and could easily move around, cutting through gardens and backyards without arousing suspicion. This way, I became a secret news carrier. All the Jews had already turned in their radios; consequently, we were cut off from any official information, except for my grandfather, who had a hidden radio on which he listened to the BBC every day. He had me learn the news reports by rote so I could recite them to the local pharmacist, Mr. Szinetár, a member of the resistance, and he, in turn would disseminated the information to others.

I was also told to play with the children near the airport and count the number of German planes, while my brother was assigned to the train station to count the trains and find out the schedules.

We became important links in the underground network.

In 1942, my father was conscripted into the Hungarian forced labor battalion. Previously, since Jews could no longer own their own businesses, he had sold his business, pro forma, to a trusted employee. For about two years that he served, he was able to pay an occasional visit home, but in 1944, he was transported to Poland.

Grandfather was very involved in assisting the Polish refugees by finding them safe houses, supplying them with financial help and false identities. His house became a document factory. We had samples of documents to copy. We provided passports and birth certificates, as well as blank documents that needed to be filled in. We even managed to get photographs to match the new owners. Although I had not yet attended school, I drew well and learned to forge signatures by tracing them. The original documents were placed on a piece of glass, under which was placed a candle, and the "to-be" forged documents on top of that, so I was able to trace the signatures needed on the forged documents. It was the forerunner of a light-box. Official-looking stamps were at hand. Pictures were affixed and then, under cover of darkness and across fences, I was sent to deliver the day's production to the pharmacist. Although I understood the secrecy of the operation, I didn't grasp the danger to which I was exposed.

Following the 1944 German occupation of Hungary, the Jewish population in the countryside was swiftly moved into ghettoes and, within weeks, deported to concentration camps, mostly to Auschwitz. We were spared the ghetto, but were put under house arrest because my mother's false Christian papers had aroused the suspicion of the authorities. We had to watch the town being emptied of Jews. Luckily, the policeman who guarded our house was kind and helpful. Then, my mother was suddenly arrested and we, children, were left on our own.

I wanted to see my mother and take a small pillow to comfort her. The policeman at the door told me where to find her. I sneaked into the jail and saw my mother and others behind bars. I could see she had been beaten. With some effort, I was able to push the pillow through a gap, but as I was leaving, a gendarme caught me and began to beat me viciously on my head and face with his rifle butt. He would surely have killed me had the town's police captain, who was a friend of my father's, not happened by. He rescued me and took me to the hospital. I had sustained serious injuries—I had a fractured skull, and my face was a bloody mess. To this day, I still carry visible scars. The hospital couldn't keep a Jewish patient, and so after emergency treatment, my head covered in bandages, the police captain took me home. When he learned of my mother's arrest, he immediately issued a release order, and she came home. Soon after, all the Jews in the jail were shot.

Our police guard informed us of the imminent deportation of all remaining Jews in the area and advised us to leave immediately.

My mother packed a small bundle of necessities and all the money she had, then we headed for the mountains. It was the late spring of 1944. I had fond memories of the majestic, beautiful Carpathian Mountains, where I remembered family excursions of hiking and bicycling. But those mountains were now a forbidding place where we had to survive for ten months without proper clothing, food, water, or adequate supplies. The area was a sparsely populated wilderness with few homes separated by many miles from each other. The poor, illiterate Romanian goat herders who lived there barely even knew about the war. They were kind and hospitable to us, shared their food and small huts, but my mother didn't dare stay longer than one night in any place. We were constantly on the move and slept in caves or on the open ground. We never knew when we would find a human habitation or get provisions. We walked and climbed relentlessly in rain and snow and suffered from terrible thirst and hunger. I contracted malaria from drinking polluted water and had recurrent malaria attacks for many years. Winter arrived early in the mountains. We walked in deep snow in our summer shoes, so I suffered severe frostbite on both feet.

Finally, the following spring brought liberation, and we returned to Zilah. My grandparents had survived, and we were waiting and hoping for my father's return. A few postcards had come from him from Poland, the last one arriving on Easter 1945.

In spite of the thorough search I undertook, I only learned about my father's fate in 2005. Apparently, he was in several concentration camps in Poland and then Germany. He died on April 30th 1945, five days before liberation. He would have been thirty-eight years old on May 1st. Although I was only seven or eight when I last saw him, I have very vivid memories of him and can never reconcile myself to his loss.

Budapest 1959

New York 1992

Name: Tutzi Marton

Born: Bucharest, Romania, 1936

Paternal Grandparents	**Maternal Grandparents**
Grandfather	**Grandfather**
Antoniu Marton	Alexander Roth
B: Ormezo, 1882	**B:** Poland, 1887
D: Unknown	**D:** Zalau, Transylvania, 1947
Grandmother	**Grandmother**
Rachel (née Salomon)	Susana (née Molnár)
B: Vaskapu, 1882	**B:** Táutu-Negru, Transylvania, 1890
D: Ciumarna, Transylvania, year unknown	**D:** Oradea, Romania, 1977
Father	**Mother**
Samuel Marton	Terezia (née Roth)
B: Unguras, Transylvania, 1907	**B:** Táutu-Negru, Transylvania, 1912
D: Deportation, 1945	**D:** Oradea, Romania, 1996

Prewar

My family lived in Bucharest. There were two of us children, my older brother Alex and I. I was "Daddy's little girl". In 1940, while visiting family in Transylvania, Hungarian forces occupied the area, and we were unable to return home. My father then started a car service business in Zilah. In 1942, my father was taken to a labor camp, while the rest of us were placed under house arrest.

War

From the spring of 1944 to April 1945, we were in hiding in the Meszes Mountains. My name in hiding was Rozsika (see my story).

Postwar

In 1954, I graduated from high school in Oradea, Romania (formerly Nagyvárad, Hungary). In 1957, I moved to Budapest, where I married Ervin Meszesi, another Hidden Child. In Budapest, I completed my studies at the Academy of Journalism. Following that, I worked for the Romanian newspaper *Foaia Noastr* for several years.

To the Present

After divorcing in 1972, I immigrated to the United States, settled in New York, and began to paint. In 1990, I started making miniature wire sculptures and intricate jewelry designs. I now divide my time between Budapest and New York City.

Budapest 1944, with parents and grandmother

Erika Montalbano

Blood for Trucks

After sixty-two years, I visited The Place. It took me until now to be able to speak or write about it.

This day will stand out in my memory for a long as I shall live.

It was October 15, 1944.

At the time, we were already in a designated "Jewish House " and my life was not too bad -as far as I was concerned. I was ten years old.

My whole extended family lived in my grandmother's large apartment; there were six families in six rooms. On that day, the Regent of Hungary, Miklos Horthy, proclaimed on the radio that he had come to the decision, not to be part of the Axis Powers anymore. The next morning, German soldiers came to our house and ordered us to the basement. The speech was short and to the point: we would be killed before Stalin could come to our rescue.

On the street we found the Jews from all neighboring houses and the Hungarian mob, ready and waiting for us with sticks and insults. My father held me close; ready to take the blows for both of us. My mother guarded my sickly grandmother.

After an eternity passed, we were gathered in a courtyard and told to stand with our hands high up, facing the wall, with a machine gun set up behind our backs. The whole neighborhood was there, a couple hundred condemned Jews. I asked my father if it would hurt to die. He said "No", but then he told me to fall down when the shooting started, to play dead, and he would stand behind me to catch the bullets.

"After all is clear, run away. Run to your aunt's house."

I recall not answering, but thinking, "I'd rather die here, with all of you."

We spent the day there, about fifteen hours. Most of that time I watched the shadows on the wall in front of me, looming larger and larger as the sun set, and when night fell, we all lay down on the hard stone of the courtyard.

The Germans guarded us in full armor. Their steel helmets glistened in the dark evening, and their shadows grew enormous on the wall behind me. I was cold, hungry, scared, and very wet because we were not allowed to relieve ourselves.

Soon, we were gathered up by the German soldiers who were armed to the teeth; a sad row of marching Jews — with a Tiger tank at our backs.

We were led to a synagogue nearby— a few shots rang out when a blind man tried to feel his way around. Jewish forced labor army members brought us soup once a day, risking their lives to be with us—we who were about to face the trains to the death camps.

Four days passed, sitting, sleeping on the wooden benches, and then, we were told to leave— leave very fast — go home!

We still wonder why they let us go.

It must have been the short-lived agreement of "Blood for Trucks".

Circa 1970 New York

New York 2007, with husband, Dominic

Name: Erika Montalbano (née Stein)

Born: Budapest, 1934

Paternal Grandparents	**Maternal Grandparents**
Grandfather	**Grandfather**
Samuel Stein	Marcus Har-Lev
B: Place unknown, 1870	**B:** Vienna, 1870
D: Auschwitz, 1944	**D:** Vienna, cca 1928
Grandmother	**Grandmother**
Julia (née Weiss)	Fanny (née Koch)
B: Place unknown, 1872	**B:** Vienna, 1872
D: Budapest, May 1945 (from typhoid fever contracted from a relative recently returned from a concentration camp)	**D:** Budapest ghetto, February 1945 (Just after Liberation)
Father	**Mother**
József Stein	Paula (née) Har-Lev
B: Budapest, 1899	**B:** Budapest, 1904
D: Budapest, 1979	**D:** New York, 1989

Prewar

Both my parents were born in Budapest, but my mother and her family went back to live in Vienna where they originated from, and Mother lived there until she got married and moved back to Budapest.

She and I often visited, going on a big boat, until the Anschluss. In 1939, my Grandmother came to live with us while my Mother's siblings escaped to Israel (then Palestine). My Father's parents came to Budapest from a Schtetl somewhere in the Carpathian mountains, but they also conversed in German.

I was bilingual until I came to the States, when I added English to my other languages.

My father was in the wholesale textile business.

I went to a Jewish elementary school.

War

When the German army marched in to Budapest, we should not have been there because we knew enough from our own family in Vienna. We had also met people who had escaped from the German mass-killings in Poland. One such family was supported by my family.

We were lucky to have the means to bribe some people to hide us, but in the end he greatly disappointed us. I was very fortunate to have the security of having my Mother with me the whole time.

Postwar

After the Holocaust, I was a student in the *zsido gimnázium* (Jewish high school), where I studied for seven years. For my last and eighth year, my father insisted that I enroll in a secular school to further my studies, and I had to leave my school and friends. Since I was good at math, I was accepted at Budapest Technical University. I married an assistant Professor of Mechanical Engineering.

We, the students, were the first to take part in the uprising in 1956 October, and a month later we escaped. We spent three months in Vienna, where I was a German-Hungarian translator for the Jewish Agency, which helped us and our fellow Jewish refugees.

My husband had an American uncle who helped us immigrate to the United States in 1957, where my daughter was born that same year. I worked for several engineering consultants in the United States, where people did not like or accept female engineers.

I joined the Port Authority, where, after a while, they accepted me and made me feel almost equal to the male colleagues. I worked there as an architect, and I met my second husband, who was Chief Engineer of construction.

I was privileged to have worked at the World Trade Center, in those magnificent towers. I had a small office that overlooked the Statue of Liberty, and I watched the big ocean-liners being greeted by the Coast Guard.

It was my fate to be there during the February 1994 terrorist attempt to destroy the World Trade Center.

A year later I retired.

I live on the Upper West Side at Manhattan's Lincoln Square.

Budapest 1934 with Mother and Father

Suzanne Nash

IRONIES AND ABSURDITIES

One would think that since I was already a young teen at the time of the German occupation of Hungary, I would remember everything well, and I do to a large degree—except one thing. I don't remember my name! I don't remember the name I went by. The name that saved my life, the one that was printed on our false identification in case anyone questioned us.

After the German occupation of Hungary in 1944, my father, an attorney, procured papers for us and sought a safe hiding place.

He had a client named Margit, a well-rounded, blonde, blue-eyed, typically Hungarian looking country type young woman, who proved to be an excellent entrepreneur. She imported and exported goods and more than made up for her husband's modest army officer's salary.

Her husband was fighting on the Russian front, and she was living alone in their large apartment. She suggested to my father that we should move in with her and provide her with financial compensation as well as favorable testimony after the war—if we survived. Her husband had witnessed terrible atrocities against civilians by the German/Hungarian armies and was concerned about the looming Soviet occupation and his own safety as a former officer. My father thought this a good proposal and started making preparations.

These preparations included taking provisions to our prospective new home. This had to be done piecemeal, during the short periods between curfews, so as not to attract attention.

A large part of these provisions was liquor: rum, cognac, *slivovitz*, and *barack* (strong Hungarian plum and apricot brandies). The Russians were already preparing the siege of Budapest, and we knew that when food supplies dried up, liquor would become legal tender on the black market.

By the time the three of us—mother, father and I—moved into Margit's maid's room, everything was in place.

Shortly thereafter, an olive skinned and dark-eyed young woman appeared in the apartment, ready to move in. Margit introduced her as her sister fleeing from Eastern Hungary. My father was concerned because her papers were not in good order; however, he felt he was in no position to complain. Another short period later, an older couple also moved in and were introduced as Margit's "father and step mother", also fleeing from the Eastern Front. One look at them told us that they were Jews. Furthermore, they didn't speak the country dialect of eastern Hungary. We knew they were from Budapest. Again, their papers were not in good order, and this time my father really became quite concerned. We didn't dare go to the shelter during bombing raids, fearing the regular "checks" that the Arrow Cross conducted in the shelters. If one person was suspect, all were in danger.

Then the final straw! Margit's husband came home. He had deserted! This time my father couldn't contain himself, and he took Margit aside to explain the danger we were now all subjected to. He told her that, had she said something earlier, he could have provided the older couple and the young woman with good forged papers. "I could have helped," he said, "why didn't you tell me that you were hiding other Jews?"

Margit then confessed. This really was her father. He had been married to a Gentile woman, Margit's mother, who had died young, after which he had remarried, taking a Jewish woman as his wife and with whom he had a second daughter, Margit's dusky sister!

We were all in shock. Margit was half Jewish!

The husband, Gyula, was another problem. Deserters were shot on sight. He, however, breezily dismissed all concerns.

"Don't worry," he said to my father, "we're all going to be perfectly safe."

"How?" inquired my father incredulously.

"We'll throw a party. You have lots of liquor. There's an Arrow Cross headquarters across the street. They are all my friends. Once they drink your liquor, they'll be your friends forever."

My father was more than skeptical, but Gyula went ahead and invited the local Arrow Cross leader and his henchmen, who were more than happy to come and party. They came and whooped it up, drinking, singing, and making a great deal of noise that no one in the building dared to complain about.

A few days later, we were asked if they could have another party. Of course they could! And then another one! We were indeed safe!

With the Arrow Cross coming in and out of the apartment, everyone in the building was terrified of us.

The irony of all this was that when we finally dared to use the shelter, which the local Arrow Cross no longer checked, everyone, especially a family whom we recognized as Jews with false identifications, kept as far away from us as possible. Fear written all over their faces!

*****

Unfortunately this relatively safe situation did not last, nor was it able to save my father's life. A couple of unexploded shells at the entrance to our shelter compelled him to go out and seek an alternative place of safety for us. A few blocks away, someone recognized him and alerted a roaming Arrow Cross group, and he was summarily shot and killed. We learned of this that evening when a man came to our shelter, quite shaken after witnessing this execution and asked if anyone knew the victim, describing his appearance and clothing. We immediately recognized my father but did not dare acknowledge it; doing so would have put all of us in danger. It was a terrible shock, but we did not have the luxury of mourning. We had to focus our energies on survival. It was just days before liberation.

I remember all of this well—all except my name.

Budapest 1948

New York 2006

Suzanne with Grandchildren, 2007
Left to right Danielle, Suzanne, Emily, behind her, Benjamin, Gabriel, Nathaniel

Name: Suzanne Nash (née Zsuzsanna Lukács)

Born: Budapest, 1930

Paternal Grandparents	**Maternal Grandparents:**
Grandfather Ármin Lukács **B.** Miskolc, 1860 **D.** Kaposvár, 1928	**Grandfather** Miksa Preisz **B.** Nyitra, 1865 **D.** Budapest, 1953
Grandmother Janka (née Moreno) **B.** Szeged, 1871 **D.** Auschwitz, 1944.	**Grandmother** Róza (née Feldman) **B.** Tolcsva, 1862 **D.** Budapest ghetto, 1945
Father: Dr. Kornél Lukács **B.** Kaposvár, 1895 **D.** Budapest, 1945 (shot by Arrow Cross)	**Mother:** Erzsébet (née Preisz) **B.** Budapest, 1899 **D.** Budapest, 1973

Prewar

My mother was a young widow when she married my father, a divorced single parent raising a son. My brother, Ivan, died tragically at age nine, shortly before I was born. I was raised as an only child in privileged circumstances. My father was a prominent attorney, and my mother managed two homes and a very busy social life. I was raised mostly by German nannies and, as a result, acquired perfect fluency in German but missed having more attention from my mother. I attended the Lutheran (*Evangelikus*) grade school and continued to the *Gymnasium* of the same school, from which I graduated after the war. I grew up in a culturally enriched environment and was introduced to the theatre, art, and music at an early age.

War

The 1940s brought increasingly stringent anti-Jewish regulations, but it wasn't until the 1944 German occupation of Hungary that we really feared for our lives. Father acquired false papers for us and a hiding place in the home of a Christian client. Unfortunately, during the siege of Budapest, an unexploded shell next to our shelter propelled my father to seek new refuge. He was apprehended on the street by Arrow Cross (Fascist) thugs and was shot. My mother and I survived and had to undertake the difficult task of rebuilding our lives after liberation.

Postwar

The communist terror took over in 1947, and my mother encouraged me to leave the country. I escaped in 1949 to Austria and lived in DP camps for a year. I met my future husband, Marcel Clinger, a chemical engineer and also a survivor, in Vienna. Our son, Michael, was born in England. From there, we moved to Zurich and later to Spain. We arrived in New York in 1955, which has remained my home ever since. I worked as a controller for an insurance agency. My husband passed away in 1983, and I married Sheldon Nash in 1987.

Life to the Present

Since my retirement from business, I have been engaged in volunteer work. I now serve on the executive board as an officer of a national fundraising organization. My husband and I enjoy traveling, and I enjoy visiting my five grandchildren.

Budapest 1941, with mother

Tamas Revai

Getting Away with Murder

I hate the month of November, especially Novembers in Budapest. It is rainy, cold, and I am always shivering. It is very uncomfortable. Just like Budapest is.

November 1944 was cold. That morning, in the ghetto apartment where we used to live, it was very cold. The whole family lived in only one of the bedrooms because five other families had moved in to occupy the rest of the apartment. I was washed and dressed in warm clothing, and everybody thought my new leather coat looked perfect for the Big Escape. My mother and grandmother got dressed very warmly, and my grandmother showed everybody her new shoes. They looked like combat boots, custom-made from calf leather in the latest style. My mother checked our forged papers, and we all felt very hopeful of being able to escape from the ghetto.

Our friends in a "safe house" were waiting for us. We got through the gates of the ghetto and felt comfortable walking toward the streetcars. However, before we got to the station, someone recognized my grandmother and called the *Nyilas* (the Arrow Cross). Our papers were obviously forged, and we were forced into a long column of Jews who had also been caught outside of the ghetto. We were made to walk through the city, and the column grew as we plodded along. At one point we had to stop to allow another column coming from a different direction to merge with ours. As we were standing there, a Hungarian woman shouted that the Jews had better clothing than they had and demanded that the guards give them the good shoes and warm coats the Jews were wearing. Suddenly, a crowd swooped down on us. A woman was tearing off my grandmother's shoes; another was taking my mother's coat. Like animals, they were attacking and taking all the warm clothes off our backs. I was little; it was my ninth birthday, and hidden somewhere in the middle of the column, I was spared. I just watched, terrified, while people around me had their clothes ripped off by the mob. I was numb with fear and cold.

We were then made to walk silently toward Óbuda: my grandmother walking on the pavement without shoes, my mother without a coat.

We ended up in the "Téglagyár" (the brick factory), which was the assembly place for Jews who were to be deported to Auschwitz. We were tired, hungry, cold, and barely walking. It was mostly an open space where the bricks were left to dry and an empty building where people were cramming into to protect themselves from the cold as much as possible.

Inside the factory, each family huddled together. The ones who had arrived before us were in the middle of the building, where it was warmer, but we were on the periphery. We tried to sleep. Suddenly, about twenty feet from us, a woman started to scream hysterically. Her family tried to calm her down, but she was crying and screaming so loudly! I had never heard anything like that. It seemed like the screams of an animal.

A Hungarian guard came in and ordered her to keep quiet. But she couldn't be calmed down and continued to scream. The guard took out his revolver and shot her dead.

That has been my nightmare ever since. It is always the same. I relive the death of that woman.

The next morning, a Gentile friend of my grandfather's, Detective Kovács, arrived at the brick factory and demanded to see us. He had a warrant for our arrest, he said. The entire family was wanted for murder, he told the guards, and he showed them the warrant. He arrested us and bundled the whole family into his car, then proceeded to drive us back to the ghetto.

We spent the next two months there, through the siege of Budapest, until we were liberated by the Soviets.

Regensburg, Germany 1960

San Francisco, with Grandsons, Reis and Trevor 2007

Name: Tamas Revai

Born: Budapest 1935

Paternal Grandparents	Maternal Grandparents
	Grandfather
Unknown	Jenö Kovács (step)
	B: Mohács, date unknown
	D: 1944, on death march in Austria
	Grandmother
	Magdalena (née Lustig)
	B: Unknown
	D: 1953, Budapest
Father	**Mother**
Aladár Révai	Franciska (née Friedman)
B: Budapest, 1908	**B:** Budapest, 1914
B: Budapest, 1976	**D:** Budapest, 1993

Prewar

From 1935 to 1956, I lived at Wesselenyi utca 35, which was in the ghetto. I attended the Julianna school in the Fasor from 1942–1946 (with a break during 1944–45). I stayed in the ghetto from March 1944 to October, then hid in a hospital with my mother until we were liberated in January 1945.

Postwar

From 1947 to 1955 I attended the *francia iskola* and *Madács gimnázium* (high school). In 1950, the French school closed and became part of *Madács*. Since I was labeled a "capitalist," I could no longer attend and studied as a chef's apprentice at the Gellert Hotel in Budapest, while still studying at the *Madács* as a private student until 1955, when I went back full time and received my *érettségi bizonyitvány* (matriculation).

Between 1955 and 1956, I worked as a chef at the school of economics (Gazdasági Egyetem) and in April 1956 was named chef for the Hungarian Olympic team in Tata.

I left Hungary during the revolution of 1956 and made my way to Pforzheim, Germany, where I again worked as a chef. From there I went to Heidelberg, where I worked for the American PX while going to school to learn hotel management.

Life to the Present

I arrived in New York in 1961. I worked as a *special request chef* at the Assembly, a restaurant on West 44th Street frequented by City politicos. As soon as my knowledge of English was adequate, I enrolled in Bernard Baruch, City College, studied accounting and received my degree in 1968.

I married Loretta Zayas in 1963 and went to live in Dix Hills, Long Island. We divorced in 1985. We have two children, Erik, who became a labor and civil rights attorney, and Krystal, a pediatrician.

I have a brother and sister living in Budapest. András Revai, formerly a dean at the Zemmelweiss University, and Marianna Magyarszeki, who worked in exports.

As of 2008, I am still active in my business (I'm a CPA and CVA) and plan to retire soon.

Budapest 1942

Miriam Steinmetz

Poems and Stories
I NEVER GOT THE GOLD EARRINGS

I was only three and a half years old when the Germans entered Hungary in March 1944, so my memories are very sporadic and, I fear, probably not in chronological order. The lingering effects, however, have stayed with me since. When thinking of my early childhood, the first thing that comes to mind is hunger and cold and the fear of hanging upside down, by my feet, from a tree. My first actual memory is hearing warning shouts in the courtyard of our building, "The Arrow Cross is coming! The Arrow Cross is coming!" I ran into our apartment, relaying the message at the top of my lungs. My grandfather fell to the floor. There was a lot of commotion. A neighbor came, lifted me up onto his shoulder and took me outside. My grandfather was dead. He had died instantly of a massive heart attack. I would never get the gold earrings with the red stones that he had promised me.

During the bombing raids, I remember being in the cellar with my mother, my grandmother, and my great grandmother, whom I had named "*bableves nagymama*" ("Bean Soup Grandmother"). She always made bean soup because dried beans were all we had … and it was never enough! My father had already been called up for forced labor duty and my grandfather was dead, so there were only the women. One time, an Arrow Cross member burst into the cellar. I'm not sure what he was looking for … Jews, maybe. In any case, he spotted a wedding ring on my mother's finger and demanded it. I started crying, and he said, "Don't cry, my little dove!" That Arrow Cross punk called me his little dove! But he took my mother's ring anyway.

Some time later, my mother took me up a long flight of stairs into a large, well-lit room where there were several other children. She handed me a carrot. I loved carrots. And she left me there, alone and crying. Some nuns came for us; creatures in long black robes and huge black-and-white wimples. While they were gathering us up, an air raid warning sounded, and they ushered the older children down the stairs into the cellar, but there was no time to come back for us little ones, and we were left upstairs. The cellar was hit, and the older children all died. The rest of us were taken to the orphanage run by the nuns. It was very cold there. But there were lots of toys, especially a beautiful hobbyhorse that I longed to ride, but never did. The older children had taken charge of it and only allowed rides to those who gave them their daily portions of black bread. I always ate mine right when I got it. I was always so hungry! Now whenever I see a hobbyhorse in a toyshop window, I cringe and turn away. I don't want to see hobbyhorses.

Eventually, the nuns hid the Jewish children in a villa in the Buda hills on the Svábhegy, where the back of the house abutted onto the courtyard of an SS headquarters. When I looked out the window, I saw people hanging from trees, upside down by their feet with their hands tied together behind their backs. Dead.

Reading my mother's diary, the story becomes clearer, and the memories take shape. She had been deported to Bergen-Belsen and then liberated by the British Army. She had been in such terrible physical condition, weighing just twenty-eight kilos, that they put her in the hospital. However, she managed to get word to my grandmother that she was alive and would be coming home, and she asked my grandmother to try to find me, that she had left me with the Anglican nuns. According to the diary, my grandmother eventually found me, dirty, underweight, and head shaved because of lice. At first the nuns wouldn't relinquish me, claiming that I was an "orphan", but grandmother had come prepared with a large paper bag filled with raisins ... and I went straight for the raisins, even though I didn't recognize her. The nuns thought that I had because I went to her so readily. She became "Raisin Grandmother" as her mother had been "Bean Soup Grandmother." Bean Soup Grandmother had died of hunger in the ghetto.

My mother had written, "When I saw Marika (sic) again, she was in painful physical state. Her hair had started to grow back ... but we were both alive. The nuns had saved her ..."

My father never returned.

Winter, 1944,
Budapest Jew House

Do not be afraid my little dove
Said the man in black to me
As my mother held me tight,
In the old basement of the Jew House.
Do not be afraid now, it is only gold
I'm after. Later, I will take lives …
I already took your childhood.
No more carefree days in the park,
No more Grandpa pushing the swing
Higher and Higher.
Only a deep hunger for loving arms
To hug and love the little dove remains.
The constant dread of swinging from
The tree, dead, is what stays.

Prayer for Magda

Little siddur bound in leather
Book of prayers framed in gold
Found in the rubble of the old synagogue
I'm holding you close

Given to me long ago.
The flyleaf reads "To Magda with Love
From Mom and Dad, September five
Nineteen thirty nine"

I treasure this memento from the past,
Prayers from happier times in the life
Of a Family lost
In the fiery abyss of hate.

Illuminated by burning flames
Of Friday night candles
I think of her as I turn the pages
And softly say her prayers.

The prayer book (Siddur) was found in the rubble of the Great Synagogue in Györ, Hungary, after WWII and given to me by my father, Imre Drach, when I was seven years old.

Midnight Blues

Umbrella of midnight blue above
Pierced by brilliant lights
Windows assigned by the Unseen
For millions of souls in heaven.
One is my father's, my guiding light.
Evil tore us apart when I was small.
Did not know then; I do now
What life might have been
Had you lived.

And I'm left with the silence of the night
As I gaze at the stars,
You see me in the here and now.
Send me strength, send me love to cope
With this aching constant void
Embedded in my heart

I was nine months old when my father was up for forced labor and sent to the Eastern Front in WW II. He later perished in the winter of 1944–45.

Brooklyn 2007, with son, Leiser and Grandchildren, Chaya, Hendi-Rifke, and Shoshana

New York 2007, Miriam (R), with daughter Judy

Name: Miriam Steinmetz: (née Marika Kelemen)

Born: Budapest, 1940

Paternal Grandparents	**Maternal Grandparents**

Grandfather

Ernö Kelemen

B: Szabadka, Hungary

D: Auschwitz, 1944

Grandfather

Lengyel Miksa

B: Szombathely, Hungary, 1878

D: Budapest, 1944

Grandmother:

Matild (née Kurzweil)

B: Budapest, date unknown

D: Budapest, 1938

Grandmother

Ernesztin (née Zeissler)

B: Budapest, 1887

D: New York, 1967

Father:

László Kelemen

B: Budapest, 1905

D: Auschwitz, 1944

Mother

Hedwig (née Lengyel)

B: Budapest, 1912

D: Miami, Florida, 1985

Prewar

We lived with my extended family. My great-grandparents owned a grocery in Sárkány utca in Budapest. My mother, an only child, had grown up in a well-to-do merchant family. While she was single, each new season for her began with new ball gowns and many suitors. My father and his sister Elizabeth came from a working class family. After she married, my mother ran her father's hide brokerage, and my father was in charge of sales. I was their only child, and we lived a comfortable, happy life together.

War

My father was taken to do forced labor (*munkaszolgálat*) before my first birthday and was deported in 1944. He never returned. My mother and I lived in a "safe house" (under the protection of a foreign embassy) in Budapest at Népszinház utca 27. We lived in one apartment with my maternal great-grandmother and grandparents, my mother's cousin, and her daughter, who was the same age as I. My grandfather and my great-grandmother both died in that apartment. When my great-grandmother died, my grandmother had to place her body on a sled and pull it by herself to the cemetery.

When my mother heard that the inhabitants of the safe houses were about to be deported, she decided to hide me to keep me safe and took me to an orphanage in Buda. Her cousin refused to part from her child. They and my mother were deported to Bergen-Belsen the next day. While in hiding, I escaped death when the orphanage was bombed. At the end of the war, my grandmother found me and managed to convince the nuns to let me leave with her. My mother eventually returned from Bergen-Belsen. She weighed only seventy pounds at the time. She still managed to overcome many challenges on the way, including the bombing of the train she was on and narrowly escaping rape by a Russian soldier.

Postwar

My mother was introduced to Imre Drach, a Holocaust survivor from Györ who had lost his wife and a two-year-old daughter in Auschwitz, as well as his businesses and his home. They married. Imre Drach adopted me. They subsequently had another daughter, Zsofika, and the family eventually moved to Sopron, near the Austrian border. Later, I went to Budapest to continue my education and was there in 1956 when the revolution broke out. I was sixteen years old and alone, while my parents and younger sister took advantage of the open border to escape to Austria, but my grandmother stayed in Sopron. Ironically, in Budapest, I was back in the basement of the same so-called safe house where we had lived in 1944, before I became a 'Hidden Child'. After a harrowing journey from Budapest to Sopron, my grandmother and I escaped from Hungary to Vienna. By this time, my parents had arrived in New York and were trying to track us down. We were finally reunited in New York in 1957.

Life to the present

We moved to the South Bronx, and I enrolled at the Bronx School of Science, one of the special high schools of New York City. My first marriage was to an Orthodox man, although my family in Budapest had been neolog. It was a great and difficult change for me. Perhaps becoming Orthodox was my way of lessening my childhood memories. Years of hard work in our jewelry store followed while bringing up our children: my daughter, Judy, and my son, Leiser (Robert). Eventually, we divorced, and two years later, I married my current husband, who already had three daughters and twenty grandchildren of his own. I now have three granddaughters of my own. In the meantime, I became a licensed real estate broker. It has been a long road and rocky road from the basement of the Jewish house to the freedom of New York.

1957, After arrival to the US, with mother, father, and sister, Shoshi

Back from deportation 1945

Zahava Szász Stessel, Ph.D

STATIONS ON THE ROAD OF LIFE

We had been coming to the train, day by day, for the last six weeks. Two teen-age sisters who were waiting for parents that never arrived. We were told gently that we should continue on with our lives, but we didn't know how.

Another train in Abaújszántó, a small town in northeastern Hungary, had carried us away from the same station a bit more than a year before. We were at that time, my mother, father, grandmother and grandfather, who was a wounded war veteran, me, my sister Erzsike, and the rest of the town's Jewish population. After just the two of us remained, aged thirteen and fourteen—following selection in Auschwitz, only the hope that we would all meet again at home made us continue. We had the fortitude to live through Bergen-Belsen, through slave labor in Markkleeberg, Germany, and to endure the Death March march to Theresienstadt in the spring of 1945.

We had the option to go to Sweden or possibly to the United States at the end of the war, but we just wanted to return to that magical place called "home." After a tortuous journey upon crowded trains with the peril of Russian soldiers hungry for women, we finally arrived in Budapest. There, like other survivors, we received from the Joint (American Jewish Joint Distribution Committee) some cash as first aid. We could have spent the money on clothing, food, or other items, but we wanted to save it. Arriving in Abaújszántó, we hurried to pay off the remaining taxes on our house at 7 Szapolyai Tér. Still believing in fairy-tale endings, I even saw my mother's smile of approval and being proud of us. After that noble act, we began to settle into weekday normality. We were living in a small room that was emptied for us in our house, while the rest of the house remained occupied by strangers. Our hearts and minds just couldn't adjust. We received lunch at the Jewish communal kitchen and arranged our day according to the trains' arrival schedule.

In a small railway station it was easy to spot a newcomer. When I noticed someone in the distance who looked uncertainly around, my heart accelerated until the traveler became identifiable. One day, Aladár Grűnspan, the father of my childhood friend, came home. It took a while until we identified each other, and then we both had the questions and no answers. The meeting was painful for all of us. We were thinking of our father, while Mr. Grűnspan missed his daughter.

By the end of the summer of 1945, most of those who had survived had returned or were heard from, yet we still waited faithfully for the train arrivals. On one of the gray rainy days, we stayed inside the station. Suddenly, we heard our name called and rushed outside. There stood a young man who introduced himself as a relative. His name was Zeev Shahar. He had lived in Palestine during the war. Now he returned as an emissary to organize groups for illegal immigration, as under the British mandate, immigration was severely restricted. Visiting the area, Zeev had decided to ask about our family. We were delighted to meet Zeev, and he was prepared to take us on the next train to Budapest. We got scared—we were not ready to give up our dreams and the world of our parents, the only one we knew. It took some more weeks of frustration and hopelessness until we didn't even go to the train station. We could no longer take the daily disappointment. Meanwhile, two of my classmates, one who had returned with her mother and the other whose father came back, left the town. Not one of Erzsike's classmates had survived.

We stayed at home in that small room, formally a bedroom, which was packed with memories and unfulfilled expectations. Reaching a final low point, after spending a day inside being just sad, we decided to let that fateful locomotive carry us again away from Abaújszántó, the place of our birth. We left behind our dreams to ever see grandmother Róza, grandfather Náthán, and mother Margit-Mariska-Miriam again. For my father, Sándor Szász, we still nourished a hope of meeting. I didn't know then that, thirty years later, I would be back, time and again, to write the history of Abaújszántó and its Jewish community, and that I could never say a final good-bye.

We followed the address Zeev had given us and arrived at *Mikéfe*, near Budapest, which was a former agricultural school established by the Hungarian-Israelite Agricultural Association. After the war it served as a Hachshara, or preparation, usually for agricultural work, prior to settlement in Palestine.

Still tied by a thousand knots to Abaújszántó and the past, we entered the first of the many stations to a new reality. Zeev introduced us to the group, and after that, like the other orphans, we were on our own. The girls were lovely, and we found our place right away among them. We were all Hungarians, and almost every one of us had remained alone after the war. We all had mutual plans and aspirations for a new world that had started to open up for us. We were teenagers who were finally given the freedom to be young and cheerful. We made fun even of the cooking. We were mostly equally ignorant, as none of us knew how to cook. Boys and girls worked together in the kitchen. The food was edible only to a certain degree. We had big soup pots and we, who never cooked at home, were faced with the daunting task of serving food for twenty-five hungry teens. There were girls who had some experience, so they arranged the menu and we the workers executed the plan.

The choices were usually made according to the ingredients available. One day, we were really down on supplies. As we looked around, we only found flour, eggs, and some jam. The girls decided the best would be to prepare *nokedli* (small dumplings). Hungarians have a number of dishes of unleavened flour and egg dough, boiled and served separately or in soups and casseroles. These dumplings are often substituted for regular side dishes, such as noodles, potatoes, or rice. In soup, they replace noodles. If the dumplings are added to chicken seasoned with paprika or Hungarian goulash, they absorb the sauce. This type of dough is easily prepared at home and the dumplings may be made in different sizes and shapes, according to the firmness of the dough. Leftovers can be served in many ways, too: fried with onion or cabbage, wrapped in fried breadcrumbs to be served warm with cold sour cream, sprinkled with sugar and cinnamon, and in many other ways. Our plan was to prepare the dumplings and season them with jam. It seemed a good idea, only we didn't know the required measurements and hadn't realized how much time and patience was needed for the preparation.

Manci, who knew a bit more than us, put the flour—which we had plenty of—in a bowl. She added eggs, water, and salt and mixed them with the flour. She continued till a soft dough was formed, adding more water as needed. Meanwhile, we boiled salted water in two large pots. Manci put a few spoons of the soft dough on a flat plate. We had to cut this dough with a knife into narrow strips, about the size of a large bean, and drop them into the boiling water that we stirred from time to time so the small pieces of dough shouldn't stick together. All along, the process of adding and mixing continued. After the last addition, the dumplings had to boil for about ten minutes, and then drained under cold water in a sieve. When they were ready, just like noodles, we served them with apricot jam.

We started the job enthusiastically, with high energy. The girls and boys worked in a circle around the two big pots of boiling water. It was fun for a while, until we started to get bored and asked for a break. Not knowing the right amounts Manci added too much water, but then more flour was needed to absorb it. The process became like the oatmeal in the children's story that continued to gush until the magic word stopped the flow; only we didn't have a magic way to end it quickly. Those who were hungry started to eat whatever was ready. As long they were small, the dumplings were tasty. The reinforcement crew wasn't as patient as we were, however. They dropped larger and larger pieces into the pot, just to get rid of the dough. The sizes grew from beans to walnuts, which hardened like small stones and almost broke our teeth, but we spread large amounts of peach jam on top of the dumplings and finished them with jokes and pleasure. While we were eating, others in the kitchen still toiled with the unending supply of dough. Finally, they just made the dumplings as large as oranges. Not knowing what else to do with them, the boys started to play ball, so we had to get out of their way. The incident with the unrelenting dough became a bonding experience. Years later, whenever we tried to recall the places where we had been together, we just had to mention the story with the dumplings and it brought us right back, with an avalanche of jokes, to *Mikéfe*. Besides cooking, we also had programs and educational activities. We were learning to work in the fields in preparation for life in Israel.

In the evening, we took walks in the green fields, and it was the first time we went out with boys. Except for one or two of the girls, who were rumored to have kissed a boy, our flirting was innocent. We were young, but there were some older boys who were ready to go out seriously. I met a good-looking boy called Gyuri from my neighboring town. He was among the first to greet us and was happy that we came from Abaújszántó, where he had close relatives. One evening, I went with Gyuri to walk among the trees close to our lodgings. Gyuri was an outgoing, interesting boy, and he seemed to be fond of me. Yet I had a hidden prejudice, carried from home, which prevented me from becoming closer to him. The relatives Gyuri mentioned were lower class people, who dealt with horse trading, and had a bad reputation. Despite my attraction and positive emotion, I knew that my parents would find Gyuri objectionable, "below our standard". Today, I judge a person by his merit, but then I was still a member of Hungarian society with its inherited class system. As I was struggling with my heart and conscience, Gyuri was called to leave on an *aliyah* or immigration to Palestine. I did not meet him again.

We were living together as young people with no chaperone, yet there were no sexual encounters between boys and girls. It is amazing how disciplined and reserved our relationships were. A kiss was the farthest a boy would go. There were some rumors about a couple, but they were the exceptions, and nobody approved. We did put energy into all kinds of innocent games and mischief. One favorite joke was to put a pail of water on top of the door, so when the unsuspecting victim opened it, he received a shower. It was a great time to return to life, even though the door to our room had to be locked because we feared attacks from Russian soldiers looking for women. We were happy, and none of us talked about the past. Later, when the group dispersed, I found out who we really were and that many of the boys had suffered greatly, even though they were not in the camps. Belonging to that group of young people in *Mikéfe*, with whom we continued our journey to Israel, was the best medicine. We lived in a carefree atmosphere with a bright future on the horizon. Surviving together, my sister and I became very close. Boys complained that they could never find Erzsike, who was very pretty, alone. Despite the protest, we knew we were no longer holding hands as tightly as we had in the camps and through liberation. Compared to my friends whose fate led them to live with relatives or to be adopted by well-meaning people, we had an easier time. Integrating into new family units, those war-torn teenagers were expected to return speedily to normal life and its routines, which made it more difficult for them to adjust and recover. After about two months in *Mikéfe*, the awaited call for getting on the road arrived. We packed our belongings, which included, besides clothing, two of my mother's candelabras, an oil painting made when I was four years old, and grandfather's Kiddush cup, which we recovered in Abaújszántó. We also had some photographs, a drawing of Erzsike standing by the machine in Markkleeberg that an inmate made of her, and a number of other little mementoes. It was night as we traveled to the border by truck. When we embarked, they ordered us to leave our suitcases behind. We were told they would be waiting for us on the other side of the border. It was pitch dark as we followed the guide through a narrow passage, crossing into Slovakia. Reaching the desired location, the guide left. We asked about the truck and our belongings, but there was no answer. We were inconsolable. Hungary had robbed us of our last sentimental values and possessions. Hundreds of years of my ancestors' labor, our home and stores, were all taken. We left Hungary with our lives and the clothes we wore. We were not even able to keep a photograph of our grandparents! We were so downhearted. Erzsike and I refused even the refreshments that we were offered to comfort us. Then, after a while, friends from the group came to tell us that it was time to celebrate the successful beginning of a new life. "Let's join the dance," they said, and we did

Israel 1947, Zahava and Sister Hava

New York 2004

Name: Zahava Szász Stessel, PhD (née Szász Katalin)

Born 1930, Abaújszántó, Hungary

Paternal grandparents
Náthán Szász
B: Hernád Kercs, Hungary, 1869
D: Auschwitz, 1944

Maternal grandparent
József Markovics,
B: Kiskut, Transylvania, 1853
D: 1937

Grandmother
Roza (née Reinitz)
B: Gönz, Hungary, 1873
D: Auschwitz, 1944,

Grandmother
Regina-Rivka (née Wolf)
B: Leken, Slovakia, 1857
D: 1938

Father
Sándor Szász,
B: Abaújszántó, 1896–1900?
D: Auschwitz, 1944

Mother:
Miriam (née Markovics)
B: Sátoraljaújhely, 1903
D: Auschwitz, 1944

Prewar

My name is Zahava Stessel, and the teenager I hide is Katalin Szász, who was born in a small town between Miskolc and Kosice in eastern Hungary. Our house had a long backyard with flowers, lilac bushes, and apartments for our grandparents and us. My father's clothing shop and grandfather's meat store were in front of the building.

We were two sisters, Erzsike, the younger, and I, Katalin, who grew up in a warm family environment. We had our grandparents' fullest attention, as my father was an only child. In the summers we traveled with our mother to Sátoraljaújhely to visit her parents.

This peaceful, country childhood gradually began to face increasing enmity.

War

By the age of fourteen, in May 1944, I was on the train to Auschwitz, locked in the windowless boxcar with my parents, grandparents, and Erzsike.

Only my sister and I survived Auschwitz, Bergen-Belsen, and Markkleeberg.

Postwar

Searching for a home, we joined the Zionist youth organization of *Mikéfe* in Budapest.

To reach Palestine, we returned to Germany and stayed in Indersdorf. In December 1946, our boat *Lanagev* sailed from Marseille and was captured at Haifa. We were deported to Cyprus.

In August 1947, we finally arrived in Palestine. There I changed my name to Zahava in an attempt to send Katalin back to Hungary, along with memories of the Holocaust.

Following a short stay in kibbutz Heftziba, I studied at the agricultural school of Ayanot. There I spent the War of Independence in 1948, learning to use a gun and serving in night patrol.

In 1949, I married another Auschwitz survivor, Meier Stessel. Our daughters, Miriam and Yonit, were born in New York, where we moved in 1957. At the age of twenty-seven I finally obtained my high school diploma and entered Brooklyn College. After receiving an MLS, I worked at the New York Public Library on Fifth Avenue and 42nd street, in Manhattan. Studying at night, I earned a PhD at New York University. My book, *Wine and Thorns in Tokay Valley, Jewish Life in Hungary: The History of Abaújszántó,* was published in 1995 by Fairleigh Dickinson University and Associated University Presses. The publication of my second book, *Hungarian Jewish Women in an Airplane Factory, Markkleeberg, Germany,* is scheduled for release in 2008.

Life to the Present

I am still chasing that elusive, dashing time. Alliance with the past presses me to write of that era, while commitment to the future calls me to tend more to my grandchildren. They are Israel –Dov, Ella-Tsofia, and Yarin in Israel; Keshet, Joshua, and Rakefet in the United States.

Gabor, with parents. Budapest 1944

Gabor Vermes

THE SIEGE

It was Christmas Eve, 1944. At age eleven, I was in a children's home in Buda. We were all Jewish children, hidden by the Swiss Red Cross under false names, pretending to be refugees who fled the advancing Soviet Army. The Swiss Red Cross covered all the expenses, but the man in charge was Gabor Sztehlo, a Lutheran pastor who managed to save the lives of a thousand Jewish children living in thirty homes. He was a wonderful man who put his own life on the line by doing what he perceived was his Christian duty.

The young boys and girls thrown together came from a variety of social backgrounds, but the common danger that we were all well aware of molded us into a cohesive unit. Even spoiled only children from upper-middle-class families, like myself, behaved like little soldiers, never shedding a tear or whining, even though we had no idea about the fate of our parents.

We played games, and the few adults in the home taught us various subjects.

Christmas Eve was the last peaceful day before the Russians who surrounded Budapest launched their major offensive, and a bloody siege began. None of us were converts, but the home was run by a Lutheran pastor, and so we put up a large Christmas tree and sang Christmas carols. The Red Cross distributed boxes full of candy, which most of us devoured that very evening. The adults asked us to provide some entertainment. I volunteered and produced the first and last play of my life. Much as we all repressed our memories of previous happy family lives, those memories bubbled very close to the surface. The proof of this was my so-called play. The only thing I remember about it was that some of the young actors and actresses on the stage pretended to be fathers and mothers, while others played their children. The "plot" consisted of their having dinner. Though I knew absolutely nothing about realism in theater at the time, real dinner was served to the players. For several long minutes, the audience heard nothing but the clattering of utensils and the chewing of food. Of course, I, the author, was also on the stage, and as far as I remember, I thoroughly enjoyed myself. I am not so sure that the same was true of hungry kids in the audience as the performance preceded dinner for all. But we were nevertheless as happy as we could be under the circumstances.

The next day we were bombarded by artillery, and the attacking Russian soldiers literally stopped in the garden of our villa; we became the frontline, and survival became our prime preoccupation.

CUPI

There has been a wide range of reactions through history on the part of Jews to oppression and persecution. At one extreme, we could find open rebellion, such as the Warsaw Ghetto uprising in 1943, at the other, quiet submission. There are, however, many kinds of reactions between these extremes. A quite understandable one is a flight- to-fantasy-land, an escape to transcendental or even mystical arenas that often seek deliverance from oppression and persecution by waiting for the Messiah. Such a Messiah does not necessarily have to be religious figure, as to many Jews, Karl Marx, who brought forth messianic hopes for a better and oppression-free future was. Other such escapes can be devoid of both religion or politics with the simple but powerful aim of bringing some psychic relief. I would count the vast number of Jewish comics and their grateful audiences in this category, as well as some artists, such as whimsical Marc Chagall.

In 1944, at the Jewish house, age eleven, I too became engaged in my own fantasies without, of course, consciously knowing why I was doing it. Actually, I was not alone but together with other boys of roughly the same age. We played cops and robbers, but considering the times, we were resisting the German occupiers, who were our sworn enemies. All this appeared harmless until Cupi arrived. Cupi was the nickname of a seventeen-year-old boy who became our leader. We did not quite realize that Cupi was mildly retarded, otherwise he would never have played with us kids. On the other hand, our worshipful attitude toward his unquestionable leadership must have been most gratifying to him; we would have followed him to the end of the world. We held our meetings, most appropriately, in some underground spot.

One evening, in a hushed tone of voice, Cupi told us that he was about to get hold of a single hand grenade. Suddenly, our resistance against the Germans took tangible shape and form, and we were ready, so we thought, to face down the enemy: with a single hand grenade. We entrusted our fearless leader with questions of when and how.

One day, Cupi disappeared, together with his parents, which saved us from a big embarrassment, and it led to the sudden disappearance of illusions and fantasies beyond the vanishing point. Without him, there was to be no hand grenade, and our game remained just a game … Thank God!

Texas 1957

New York 1992

Name: Gabor Vermes, PhD

Born: 1933, Budapest

Paternal grandparents	Maternal grandparents
Grandfather	**Grandfather**
Zsigmond Vermes	Geiger (Hegedüs) Vilmos
B: Szeged, 1873	**B:** Osztopan, 1868
D: Szeged, 1937	**D:** Gyomro, 1958
Grandmother	**Grandmother**
Leona (née Benedict)	Zsofia (née Schrank)
B: Pancsova, 1876	**B:** Tardoskedd, 1872
D: Szeged, 1950	**D:** Budapest, 1955
Father	**Mother**
Dr. Andor Vermes	Margit (née Hegedüs)
B: Szeged, 1900	**B:** Budapest, 1903
D: Budapest, 1954	**D:** Budapest, 1988

Prewar

I was the only child of an upper-middle-class Jewish family. My father had a law degree but never practiced law. He was a self-taught economist. He entered the employ of the Hitelbank, one of Hungary's major banks, as a clerk, in the early 1920s but rose quite high in the bank's ranks, even though his career was derailed by a major illness in the 1930s when he spent close to two years in a sanatorium.

I had governesses and a private music teacher, and as a spoiled brat, I took pleasure in tormenting them all. Nevertheless, I was a good student at the elementary school, though what I liked best was playing soccer after school in our playground.

War

Our idyllic life came to an abrupt end when the Germans occupied Hungary on March 19, 1944. Luckily, our apartment house on Honvéd Street became a so-called Jewish house, and we did not need to move, but my maternal grandparents and two aunts moved into our apartment, which then became quite crowded. There was no school for me, we could go out to the street only during certain hours, and we had to wear the Jewish star, a humiliating experience. We, the children in the house, spent our time playing, and the older children took it upon themselves to teach the younger ones. Even this precarious existence ended when on October 15, 1944, the extreme fascists, the Arrow Cross, seized power. I remember hiding with my father in the basement of his bank for several days. (He was called to join a labor battalion several times, but each time he was let go because of a bum leg, the result of his long hospitalization in the 1930s). That hiding place was untenable, so my father and I split up. I went to my father's uncle, who had converted to Catholicism and was married to a Gentile woman. They were exempt from the Jewish laws. One of their daughters heard about the Lutheran pastor's, Gabor Sztehlo's, rescue mission, and she took me to one of Sztehlo's homes on Bogár Street in Buda. I lived through the siege there and in another house. We were not liberated by the Russians until late January, 1945. My mother, who survived with false papers, could not bear not knowing about me. She crossed the frozen Danube on foot three times, until, in early February, she tracked me down. By then, the ice cover on the Danube was beginning to thaw, but we made it back safely to Pest. Luckily, my father also survived the ordeal; a wonderful Gentile neighbor, a simple peasant woman, hid him in a basement.

Postwar

It took us some time to pick up the pieces. I went to a high school, a very good one on Trefort Street, but I was no longer the cocky little kid I used to be. Though I still liked to play, I rushed home after school and was hiding from the world, and I never went out anywhere or did anything. My interests were always geared toward the humanities, but under Stalinism, I did not want to pursue history, my real love. Rather, I entered the university as a geology major. I graduated in 1956 and was briefly employed before escaping from Hungary upon the defeat of the Hungarian Revolution, in late November 1956. By then, my mother was a widow, but with selfless heroism, she encouraged me to leave.

Life to the Present

After several months in various refugee camps, I arrived in the United States in February 1957. After a few months in New York City, I flew to Texas and got employed there in oil-exploration. I also worked in Louisiana, New Mexico, Utah, and Wyoming. It was in Louisiana where it dawned on me that I was in the wrong field, wrong for me. I started to apply to universities, and very luckily, Stanford University not only accepted me but gave me a small scholarship. I entered it in the fall of 1958. I received my master's degree in history in 1961 and my PhD in 1966. In the meantime, I got married in 1965 and had a son in 1966. I taught at San Francisco State College, UCLA, and at the University of California, Irvine. In 1972, my marriage fell apart. In the very same year, I moved to New York City for a teaching job at Rutgers University in Newark. In 1975, I married Ann, my current wife and partner in everything. I retired as professor emeritus in 2001. I am still professionally active; my biggest project is a manuscript on Hungary in the eighteenth and first half of the nineteenth centuries.

Budapest 1942

Agnes Vertes

A SIGNIFICANT MEMORY

My father was a very active Zionist when I was a very little girl, only three years old. It was a year before the Germans arrived in Hungary. I have flashes of memory from Shabbat dinners where we had strangers as guests, men with beards, very strange looking to me. My father spoke German, but they spoke a different language—I guess it was Yiddish. My father must have found out from them about the concentration camps where the Jews of other European countries were transported and that small children didn't survive in Auschwitz, but were immediately gassed when they arrived.

He decided that my sister and I should go into hiding separately. He got us false papers, which looked very authentic. I was not to be Agnes Katz, but Agnes Kovács, and I was to be Protestant. My parents told me that I should never tell anyone my real name because I might be killed. At the age of four I didn't know what it meant to be 'killed', but I was an obedient child, and if my parents thought that to be 'killed' was bad, I should listen to them.

I was drilled in the Christian prayers and told that if anybody asked where my father was, I should say, "He is on the front fighting for the glory of Germany and my mother is a refugee from Transylvania."

I was a smart little girl, and I learned fast.

One day a woman came, a stranger to me. I had never seen her before. She took my little sister with her. After that, my mother washed my hair in kerosene so I should smell like a lower class child who had just had head lice. I never did, but my clean hair and lovely curls would give me away where I was going. I had to put on different clothes, except for a knitted outfit my mother had made. This was important, because it was this outfit that helped my mother recognize me when we were reunited for a short period of time during the war.

Later, the same woman came for me, too. She was nice, but strict and told me not to cry and instructed my mother not to follow us. She picked me up and carried my little suitcase. I saw my mother following us crying even though she was told not to. She was ducking into doorways to hide from me, but I did see her. The woman, Mrs. Konus, and I took the streetcar, the number forty-nine, I still remember. As the streetcar took me away, my mother was getting smaller and smaller until she disappeared. That's when I started to cry.

The woman (I only remember her name as Konús néni) lived in a small, lower class suburb called Pestszentlörincz. Coming from my elegant home with chandeliers and Oriental rugs, it was a shock to find myself in this house with packed dirt floors and only an outhouse for a toilet. When we arrived, I saw that my sister was already there. She was only two and only said "Agika" with a big grin. Konús néni was a foster parent with eight children, all Gentile, I think, except for us, two Jews.

Mr. Szlányi, my father's friend from his university days, was a retired army colonel (I called him Rezsö Bácsi) who was a great help to us. He still wore his uniform and so he could get through the checkpoints. He visited us often and brought whatever food he could. Rezsö Bácsi even brought some chocolate sometimes, which Konus néni could trade for staples for all the children. We never did eat the chocolate, but I know that she was very kind and did her best for all of us.

The Allies were bombing Hungary all summer, and during one of the bombing raids, the hovel we were staying in was demolished. Somehow, Konus néni got word to my parents that she could no longer keep us because we had no roof over our heads. My father was hidden by Mr. Szlányi and my mother by a lieutenant who was reporting to him. She was supposed to have been a refugee from Transylvania and his mistress. My father *never* left the house because of the *razzias*, during which Jewish men were easily identified.

Konus néni insisted on accompanying us when Mr. Szlányi came to get us because she had promised my parents she would never give us away. We were walking toward the ambulance Mr. Szlanyi had procured to transport us, and he asked the three of us to wait on the sidewalk while he went to get it.

A *Nyilas* came toward us and warned us to stay on the sidewalk. As I was standing on the corner, all of the sudden a group of people appeared. They were being herded like cattle in the middle of the street. There were men, women, and even children among them, and the *Nyilas* were hitting them with the butts of their rifles and whipping them. There were many bystanders on the sidewalk yelling "*Büdös zsidok!*" ("Stinking Jews!") "*Dögöljetek meg!*" ("Drop dead!") and other epithets. They were throwing stones and debris at them. And there I stood, a little four-year-old, and, as if a light had just been turned on in my head, I realized, "So this is why I can't tell my real name to anybody. This is what would happen to me if they ever found out that my real name was not Agnes Kovács."

This horrible scene was etched in my memory forever.

*****

We were hard to place because it was already fall and the *Nyilas* were everywhere. We were finally placed in an orphanage where all the children were Jewish and probably the caretakers too. There were 100 children in the house, which had previously belonged to the mayor of Budapest.

My sister and I were the only ones to have authentic-looking papers, so when the SS or *Nyilas* came to check papers, my sister and I were always pushed ahead so our papers would be the first ones checked.

One day a particularly horrible *Nyilas* came and didn't accept that only our papers would be shown.

"We want to see everyone's papers," they said.

The blood must have frozen in the veins of the caretakers. Suddenly my sister, Zsuzsi, who was an adorable redhead, walked up to one of the men and pulled on his pants to get his attention.

"*Katona Bácsi mutasd a sapkádat.*" ("Uncle soldier, show me your cap."), she said. The *Nyilas* was taken by surprise and then began to smile. He picked her up in his arms and said to his cohort, "Could anyone but a genuine Aryan child be so adorable?"

They left without asking for our documents. My sister Zsuzsi had saved us all, although to this day she has no recollection of her heroic deed.

Graduation Hunter College 1962

Westport, Connecticut 2007

*New York 1998, Agnes and her husband Michael, at the New York Festival
where Agnes received and award for her documentary "One Out Of Ten"*

Name: Agnes M. Vertes, (née Katz)

Born: Budapest, 1940

Paternal Grandparents	**Maternal Grandparents**
Grandfather	**Grandfather**
Lipot Katz	Herman Gluck
B: Mármarossziget, 1877	**B:** Nyirbator, 1887
D: Városmajor, Budapest, 1944	**D:** Budapest, 1946
Grandmother	**Grandmother**
Cecilia (née Katz)	Maria (née Reiz)
B: Mármarossziget, 1888	**B:** Ujfeherto, 1888
D: Városmajor, Budapest, 1945*	**D:** Városmajor, Budapest, 1945*
Father	**Mother**
Armin Ernö Katz	Irene (née Gluck)
B: Mármarossziget, 1909	**B:** Nyirbator, 1914
D: New York, 1983	**D:** Fairfield, Connecticut, 2005

*Murdered in the Városmajor Hospital in Buda by the priest Kún Pater and his gang. For reference, check page 872 of *The Politics of Genocide* by Dr. Randolph Braham.

Prewar

I was born in Budapest on September 4, 1940, into a modern Orthodox family. My paternal grandparents moved to Budapest right after my father was born and had a very successful export/import wholesale business, which by the time I was born, was very profitable. My father and his brother were university educated, and his sister was educated in Switzerland. My mother came from a poor, ultrareligious family who moved to Budapest after my grandfather went bankrupt as a grain merchant. My father and his mother ran the business even after Jews were not allowed to own businesses, and they had to have a Christian "strawman". We had a cook, a maid, and a nanny and lived very well. On December 9, 1942, my sister, Suzanna, was born. My father was taken for slave labor in early 1943, but he escaped by jumping off the train. My uncles and maternal grandfather, fifty-five at the time, were all in slave labor battalions. In early 1944, my mother took my sister and me to Kiskőrös, where we had family who owned vineyards, to avoid the bombing raids.

War

My father came to get us to take us back home after the German occupation. Soon after that, my sister and I were placed with a woman who ran a foster home in Pestszentlörinc. We all had false papers, and my parents eventually went into hiding separately. My father's friend from university, who was a retired colonel in the Hungarian army, hid my father in his apartment and arranged for my mother to stay with a lieutenant who used to serve under him. In the fall, the shack where we lived with the kind woman got a direct hit, and our parents had to find a new place for us. We were then put into a home for children in Buda. We were there through Christmas and early January. When the house-to-house fighting started, the Germans took up a position on the roof of the house, and the Russians were in the garden, and they were shooting at each other. The house caught fire, and although we escaped, we were homeless for some time, living in bombed-out houses and eating snow. We ended up in a terribly crowded and dirty children's home, where we were starving. Both my sister and I were emaciated and sick with TB by the time my mother came across the Danube, on the first temporary bridge, and found us.

Postwar

I started school in September 1946 at the Jewish elementary school in Dob utca. I remember I was always late because I could not sleep at night from the nightmares I had. On May 17, 1948, my brother Leslie was born. Soon the Communists nationalized the business that my father had restarted. We were now labeled enemies of the people because our family was considered Capitalists. That meant nobody would hire my father, and if he didn't work he would be jailed as a loiterer. He finally got a job with the Chevra Kadisha. After third grade, I was transferred to the district public school because the Jewish school was no longer allowed to operate. In 1951, the government started deporting "undesirables" from the city of Budapest to backward little villages in the country. Many of these people were Jews. They had no way to earn a living. There were no health care facilities, no running water, and in some cases no electricity. Seeing this, my father, with the cooperation of the Israeli consul, got help from Jewish organizations in the United States and distributed money and medicines to these unfortunate Jews. One night, the AVH (the Hungarian secret police) came to get my father. We did not know where they took him or whether he was dead or alive. He was released during the general amnesty after Stalin died. They had almost tortured him to death, and it took years to nurse him back to physical and mental health. In 1954, I was ready to begin high school, but no school would take me because I was labeled an enemy of the people. However, I got into the Jewish Gymnasium, which was an excellent school. The Hungarian revolution of 1956 opened an opportunity for me to get away from the country where my family had suffered so much. My sister and I crossed the border to Austria and went to Vienna. My brother was sick, so my parents opted to stay behind. I supported us by trading on the black market, and when I heard they were closing the border again, I paid to have my parents brought out. We arrived together at Camp Kilmer, New Jersey, on February 23, 1957.

Life to the Present

I finished high school in the Bronx and then went to Hunter College, where I studied languages and mathematics. During my sophomore year in January 1960, I married another Hungarian Jewish child survivor from Budapest, Michael A. Vertes. We were both students and studied and worked to support ourselves. After graduation, my husband worked for the Apollo project, and I taught mathematics. In 1964, our first child, Roger, was born, and in 1968 our daughter Vivian was born. We lived in Riverdale until we built our house in Weston, Connecticut, which we moved into in January 1973. My husband got a graduate degree while working and then went to the Harvard Business School while I got an MBA. When he established his own firm, I worked with him for a few years. Later, I worked in marketing for health care companies. I was the East Coast marketing manager for a workers' compensation managed-care company. Subsequently, I was the business manager for the Connecticut-Israel Exchange Commission. At the same time, I made two documentary films about the Holocaust and won a number of awards for both. *One Out of Ten* was aired on Channel 13 and Israeli TV. *Passport to Life* has been shown as far away as Italy and Buenos Aires, Argentina. In the fall of 2005, I lost my beloved husband and at present I am teaching in Jewish schools. I have six grandchildren: three boys and three girls. I hope to make other documentary films.

Eva, Anna, Vica (Veronka) 1940

Anna Waller, PhD

A TRUE FAIRY TALE

This is my Mother's story. It is also my story because the most satisfying memories of close connection I have with my mother were those times when she would tell me her stories from the war and the concentration camp. She was my heroine, one who survived against all odds, the one who prevailed during unimaginable circumstances and was lucky enough to encounter some miraculous help at times. This story is one of those times.

I was holding onto my mother's hand. I screamed when I had to let go because the butt of a gun hit my hand, and the *Nyilas* pushed my mother into the cattle car at the Jozsef Varosi Railroad Station. I was five years old and was left with my two older sisters, ages nine and thirteen. My mother was taken to Hegyeshalom, a border station where the women were let out at night to eliminate. When they were called to return to the cattle cars, my mother decided to run away. She was hiding in the tall, dried grass when a young Hungarian soldier found her. He told her to go back into the cattle car as they were about to be handed over the SS. My mother said that he might as well kill her now, because she was not going anywhere. Three young daughters had been torn from her, and she had to go back to find them. He told her that even if he let her go, she would surely be killed before she reached Budapest and that the Germans were losing the war and it would not last much longer. He said she had a better chance of surviving if she went back to the cattle car and took her chances that way. He said to my mother: "Write a letter to your daughters, and I will find them and give the letter to them." He found an envelope in his pocket that they unfolded and my mother wrote a letter to us on it. She wrote it using his back as the "table" and by a flashlight.

My mother ended up in Ravensbruck and survived. The Hungarian soldier did indeed find us and gave us her letter:

My Darling, sweet, unforgettable children!

My Darling Terike, Irenke, Dezsoke and Pirike!* I am here in Hegyeshalom, saying good-bye to you. Here we are being transferred to the Germans, direction Germany. I believe in God so I know that I am not leaving and saying good-bye to you forever, but only for a certain period of time, and that we will all meet again shortly. Is it possible that I have so many sins that I could be torn away from my adoring children and my loving husband? No, No! I will return!! Just wait for me with love! Your tear-drenched little faces are with me day and night, and I wipe the tears off your little faces. Don't grieve for me; only take very good care of each other. My dear Veronka** give them especially motherly love until I return. Vicukam***, behave yourself, and Annikam****, pray a lot for your Mother and Father! God will listen to your darling little innocent heart!

My Darling Terikem! I beg you to go to Teleki-ter 5. The Red Cross is there and try to find the children. If you don't find them, go to Pozsonyi utca 54a, and speak to ———— and tell him that I was separated from the children on the Jozsefvarosi Railroad Station. I don't know where they were taken. I am very worried. If they were taken to the ghetto, they have to be taken out of there. They should not be left there! I hope the Red Cross will take care of it if this important, influential man speaks to them. Don't let the children be hungry or cold. Veronka knows where the money, food, and clothing are hidden. They can use my clothes as well.

The letter ends here. My mother ran out of space. Terike, as far as I recall, was the wife of my Uncle Dezsö, on my father's side. She was Gentile and had some freedom of movement. I suppose my mother directed the soldier to her house, and then somehow they were able to find us, but they were not able to get us out of the Ghetto.

---

*These are adults my mother was asking for help to find us and bring to us some food and clothing
** Oldest sister
*** Middle sister
**** Me

Greenwich Hospital, CT 1963

Syosset NY 2006

Name. Anna Waller, PhD

Born: Tarnazsadány, Hungary 1938

Paternal Grandparents	Maternal Grandparents
Grandfather	**Grandfather**
Vilmos Waller	Izidor Berliner
B: Budapest, date unknown	**B:** Domoszlo, Hungary, date unknown
D: Budapest, 1929	**D:** Auschwitz, 1944
Grandmother	**Grandmother**
Zali (née Roth)	Ethel (née Veiner)
B:Date and place unknown	**B:** Date and place unknown
D: Budapest, March 19, 1944*	**D:** Auschwitz, 1944
*The day the Germans marched into Hungary	
Father	**Mother**
Ödon Waller	Gizella (née Berliner)
B: 1901, place unknown	**B:** Domoszlo, 1909
D: Csorog, Hungary, 1946	**D:** Brooklyn, New York, 2000

Prewar

My maternal grandparents lived in Domoszlo, Heves Megye, a small village in the northern part of Hungary. They owned the village store, which supplied the peasants with clothing, materials, staples, etc. My mother stopped going to school at age sixteen to take over the management of the family store, as her parents were getting older and, being the next to the youngest child, was still home. She had four sisters.

My father's family was from Budapest. He came from a family of four boys and one girl. He was an agricultural engineer and was the overseer of one of the huge estates in Tarnazsadány, Heves Megye, owned by Grof Almásy, a member of the Hungarian nobility who lived abroad.

I was born in December 1938 in Tarnazsadány, Hungary. I am the youngest of three daughters, each of us four years apart.

Early in 1939, when the first Jewish laws appeared, my father was summarily fired and we had to leave in a very short order. This is when my family moved to Budapest. We lived there for only a short time, then we rented a farm with vineyards and tilling land about twenty-five kilometers north of Budapest, in a place called Csorog, near Vác.

My father taught my mother how to take care of the farm because she became the head of the household when he was called up for *munkaszolgálat*. She also kept our permanent address as Budapest. This was smart and lucky because it eventually saved our lives. When the Jewish laws said that all Jews had to go back to their permanent residences, we left the farm and returned to Budapest.

War

My father was called up for *munkaszolgálat* while we were in Csorog. When we returned to Budapest, we lived in my grandmother's apartment in Izabella utca 10, for about two or three months. Following that, we moved to Dohány utca 68, which became a Jewish House with a yellow star. I don't know how we got out of that house, but some notes from my mother, which I found, say we were then hidden by a Gentile family, named Gyurcsek, for about a month. The next stop was a Swedish Protected House. I believe, but I am not sure, that it was the Arrow Cross who came into the building and took us to a railroad station and deported my mother, along with all the other able-bodied women. My mother was taken to Ravensbruck, a women's concentration camp, in October 1944. We three girls, aged thirteen, nine, and five, were now in the "care" of the Arrow Cross, which meant that we were dragged, along with other children and old people, to the ghetto. Miraculously, we survived and were liberated by the Soviet army in January 1945. My memories are spotty of this period as I was very young, but they are filled with terror and close calls of being killed.

On my mother's side, three first cousins survived. Two sisters and their whole families perished. Her older sister had emigrated to Uruguay before the war, married, and had two sons.

None of my father's siblings or their families survived, except for two first cousins.

Postwar

My father survived *munkaszolgálat*, but he died of coronary thrombosis in December 1946. He was 45 years old. My mother also survived the war and returned to find us six months after liberation.

I spent about three years in a Jewish orphanage outside of Budapest, until the age of ten, when my mother did not let me emigrate to Israel, as had been originally planned. I then lived with my mother on the farm and attended elementary school in Vác and *gimnázium* in Ujpest. In December 1956, we—my mother, middle sister, and I—escaped from Hungary and spent three months in Vienna and Salzburg, waiting to be processed as Hungarian refugees. We arrived in the United States in March 1957.

My mother remarried in the 1960s, lived in Brooklyn, and died at the age of almost ninety-one.

To the Present

In the United States, I completed my undergraduate degree at night at New York University and graduated in 1967. I received a master's degree in social work in 1969 from Columbia University and a PhD in marriage and family counseling in 1984 from Columbia Pacific University. I am a psychotherapist in full-time private practice in Manhattan, and I live on Long Island. I am divorced and have one daughter, Erina, who was born in 1985.

In Memoriam

This page is dedicated to the children who did not survive to tell their stories.

THE RIGHTEOUS

 הונגריה
HUNGARY
MAGYARORSZÁG

ADAMETZ JÓZSEFNE	FERENCZY BÉNI & WIFE
ÁGOCS NÓRA	FRANKO DEZSÖ & FRANZI
ALBONYI (FARKAS) MÁRIA	FÜLÖP EMY
ANGYALOSI BELA	FÜLÖP JOHN
ANKER MÁRIA	FÜLÖP LAJOS
ANTAL JÁNOS	GÁL GYULÁNE
ANTALL JÓZSEF	GÁTI JÓZSEFNÉ (SCHULZ ANA)
APPÁN KÁLMAN & MÁRIA	GIMES ANDRÁS
ARNÓCZKY LAJOSNE	GIRNT SÁNDOR & WIFE
(DEÁK FLÓRA)	GOLOPENCZA ILLÉS
BAKONYI GÁBORNÉ	GOSZTONYI–JURISICS BORBALA
BALLA PÉTER & WIFE	GRABOVITZ JÓZSEF
BALOG ENDRE	GUTZWILLER HILDEGARD
BÁN DEZSÖNÉ (SZALMÁS ILONA)	GYULAI STEFÁN
BARTHA GYÖRGY	HANKO MÁTYÁS & TEREZ
BAUMGARTEN MIHÁLYNÉ	HEDLEY MARGIT (VÁRADI MUNCI)
(KOPP APOLONIA)	HEGEDÜS JÓZSEF & ZSUZSANNA
BELLÁK PÁLNÉ	HEGEDÜS ZOLTÁN & ERZSÉBET
	HEGYMEGY ERNÖ
	HEINTZ ELIZABETH
	HERGET JÓZSEFNÉ
	HESZ LAJOS & WIFE

Yad Vashem, Israel

Out of all of Europe's Jewish children born between 1933 and 1945, only 11 percent remained alive by the end of the WWII.

Most of these children survived the terror of the Holocaust by hiding. They survived by taking on false identities and by literally hiding: in cellars, sewers, woods, sheds, stables, bombed-out and abandoned buildings, and any shelter or burrow they could find. Many of these children were rescued and hidden by those very few incorruptible, brave, and independent souls that we now call the Righteous. In the midst of the mass hysteria and the rallying call demanding the "Final Solution", which made killers and torturers of ordinary citizens, an intrepid, defiant, and courageous few risked their own lives and refused to participate in the murder of their fellow men. Who were these valiant few? Where did they come from, and what bound them together?

They were men; they were women. Some had means, and some were poor. Some were well educated, others illiterate. Some were devoted to their religion and their belief in God, while

259

others were atheists. They came from all walks of life, from all strata of society. There appeared to be no common denominator linking them together. But there was. They believed in the sanctity of life. They refused to be corrupted. They recognized a tyrant. They had empathy and respect for their fellow man. Most of all, they were independent thinkers who saw injustice and who, despite mortal danger to themselves and their families, risked all in order to right a wrong. They were indeed "The Righteous".

We, the Hungarian Hidden Children, would like to honor the memory of those few who helped the Hungarians Jews: Those we know by name, those who remain anonymous, and those who themselves became martyrs and died heroes' deaths.

EB

The Righteous

Maria Kennedy-Babar (submitted by Judith Abrams [Grünfeld Judit])
She was instrumental in procuring Christian birth and Baptismal certificates in the name of Ilona Papp. She arranged for me to be hidden by nuns and later in her apartment in Buda, together with my grandmother and aunt. Honored at Yad Vashem.

Mater Orsolya Szudey, mother superior of the Ursuline order of nuns of Budapest, who, in 1944, was in charge of the order and collected funds for the purchase of the estate in the Hungarian countryside at Pincehely, where she hid me and other Jewish children.

Margit Végh (submitted by Evi Blaikie [Weisz Eva])
She hid us in her home, and found us other hiding places, keeping secret the fact that we were Jews, even from her family.

Vera Laska (submitted by Marika Barnett [Schweitzer Marika]),
Vera, fluent in Czech, Slovak, Hungarian, and German, guided Jews and others in danger to safety through the mountains from Czechoslovakia to safe houses in Budapest and towns to the south and to Yugoslavia.

Dr. Klinda (submitted by Judith Bihaly)
Dr. Klinda, a Catholic priest, was director of a residential girls school, *Boldog Katalin,* in the Buda hills. He began hiding Jewish children (including me) after the German occupation, later admitting Jewish women and some men and children by obtaining government approval to convert Boldog Katalin to a war factory sewing Hungarian Army uniforms. He is honored at Yad Vashem as Righteous among the Nations.

Officer Wuchte and Private Martin (submitted by Susan Bendor [Blum Zsuzsi])
(Last names unknown)
They hid three Jewish families in the cellar of the building where Officer Wuchte was in charge of a German uniform factory.

Gabor Sztehlo (submitted by Gabor Vermes) Gabor Sztehlo was a Lutheran pastor. In 1944, he was a thirty-five-year-young Lutheran chaplain attached to a hospital in Budapest. His bishop asked him to turn his attention to saving Jewish children after the Arrow Cross takeover. Sztehlo threw himself into his task with superhuman effort and courage, and he ended up saving the lives of more than one thousand Jewish children in more than thirty homes at a great risk to his own life and his family. I was in a group of children who was with him, his wife, and two children. In the 1960s, they settled in Switzerland. My best friend in hiding, Tomi Perlusz, now David Peleg a citizen of Israel, arranged for his prominent place in Yad Vashem.

Palne (Maria) Satori (submitted by Gabor Vermes), was our neighbor. She was a simple peasant woman who, out of natural goodness, obtained false papers for my parents and saved their lives. She hid my father in the cellar and brought him food every day. She received a certificate from Yad Vashem and medals from the governments of Israel and Hungary.

Members of the international diplomatic community:

Righteous Among Nations

International Red Cross (Swiss)
Friedrich Born, chief delegate
Hans Weyermann, delegate
Leopold Breszlauer
Ladislaus Kluger
George Mandel-Mantello, Hungarian Jew living in Switzerland as first secretary

General Consulate of El Salvador
Dr. Harald Feller
Dr. Peter Zurcher
Ernst von Rufs

Swedish legation
Raoul Wallenberg
Per Anger
Carl Ivan Danielsson
Lars Berg

Swedish Red Cross
Valdemar Langlet
Asta Nilsson

Spanish Legation
Angel Sanz Briz

Polish
Henryk Slavik (tortured by SS and shot in Mauthausen)

Portuguese
Carlos de Liz Texeira Branquinho
Carlos Almeida Alfonseca Sampayo

Catholic Rescuers

Monsignor Angelo Rotta, Pápal Nuncio (Ambassador) in Budapest, 1944–45
Archbishop Genaro Verolino
Lazarist priest Kohler
Dr. Margit Schlachta (Mother Superior, Social Missions Society)
Jane Haining, Scottish Mission (caught, deported, and died in Auschwitz)
Collegium Marianum
Collegium Theresianum
Lazarist Fathers
Merciful Sisters (Irgalmas nővérek)
Sophianum Institute
Baron Vilmos Apor, bishop of Györ
The Ursuline Sisters of Hungary

The Reform Church (Reformatus)

The Reverend Albert Bereczky

The Lutheran Church (Evangelikus)

The Reverend Gabor Sztehlo

Carl Lutz, Swiss diplomat

Giorgio Perlasca, Italian businessman who posed as a Spanish diplomat

The Holocaust
In Hungary and Worldwide

1930

THE WORLD WIDE DEPRESSION
HITS HUNGARY

THE NUMEROUS CLAUSUS LAW PASSED (AUG. 1920)
LIMITING UNIVERSITY ATTENDANCE BY JEWS

1933

ADOLF HITLER ELECTED
GERMAN CHANCELLOR

FRANKLIN D. ROOSEVELT IN SECOND
YEAR AS U.S. PRESIDENT

1936

JEWS SYSTEMATICALLY ELIMINATED
FROM PROFESSIONS AND DENIED
CITIZENSHIP RIGHTS.

BERLIN OLYMPICS, OVERT
ANTI-SEMITISM CURBED
FOR 3-4 WEEKS

GERMANY EXPANDS THE CONSTRUCTION
OF CONCENTRATION CAMPS

1938

"KRISTALLNACHT" IN NAZI GERMANY

1939

NAZI GERMANY OCCUPIES
CZECHOSLOVAKIA AND
POLAND

THE OUTRIGHT KILLING
OF JEWS BEGINS

JEWISH REFUGEES BEGIN
TO ESCAPE INTO HUNGARY

1940

GERMANY FAILS TO INVADE
GREAT BRITAIN

NAZI GERMANY OCCUPIES HOLLAND, FRANCE,
NORWAY AND DENMARK AND DEPORTATIONS
FROM THOSE COUNTRIES BEGINS

1941

NAZI GERMANY ATTACKS SOVIET RUSSIA.
SPECIAL NAZI SQUADS FOLLOW ARMY TO
BEGIN ORGANZIED KILLING OF ALL JEWS

JAPAN ATTACKS PEARL HARBOR

WAR IS DECLARED BY THE U.S.

1942

NAZI VICTORIES CONTINUE

WANSEE CONFERENCE ON
"FINAL-SOLUTION"

HUGE GERMAN DEFEATS AT STALINGRAD,
FIELD-MARSHALL PAULING'S 6TH ARMY
SURROUNDED AND ELIMINATED

BIG LOSSES BY HUNGARIAN ARMY
AND JEWISH LABOR BATTALIONS AT
THE DON RIVER

1943

SUBSTANTIAL GERMAN
LOSSES IN NORTH AFRICA

SOVIET ARMY BEGIN TO PUSH GERMAN
ARMIES BACK TOWARD THE WEST

1944

MARCH 19, 1944 GERMANY OCCUPIES
HUNGARY, ADOLF EICHMANN ARRIVES
WITH HIS CADRE OF "SS" MEN, 437,402
JEWS DEPORTED TO AUSCHWITZ

RAOUL WALLENBERG
ARRIVES IN BUDAPEST

SWISS VICE CONSUL CALR LUTZ, THE
SPANISH CONSUL AND THE VATICAN
NUNCIO, ALL ISSUED PROTECTIVE
"SCHUTZPASS" PAPERS TO JEWS

1945

HORTHY FAILS TO PULL HUNGARY OUT
OF THE WAR, ARROW-CROSS FASCISTS
TAKE OVER THE GOVERNMENT

HUNGARY IS LIBERATED BY
THE SOVIET ARMIES

WWII ENDS IN THE
PACIFIC

1946

HORTHY TESTIFIES AT THE NURNBERG TRIALS,
LATER RETIRING TO PORTUGAL

ARROW-CROSS LEADERS ARE RETURNED BY
AMERICANS TO HUNGARY, THEY ARE TRIED
AND EXECUTED

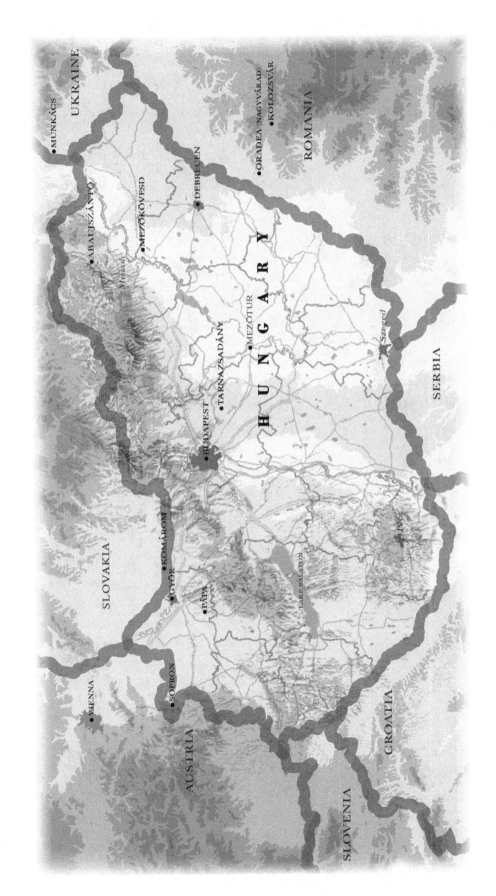

THE JEWS OF HUNGARY: A BRIEF HISTORY

By Gabor Vermes, PhD

At the time of the conquest of Hungary by the Magyars[1] in the late ninth and early tenth centuries, there were already small communities of Jews living there. We know this from the records of German-Jewish merchants who stayed with Hungarian Jewish families on the Sabbath during their return from business travel in Russia. The town of Esztergom, north of Budapest, was home to one such group of Jews.

As far as can be determined, these communities were rather poor, and their residents not well versed in Jewish liturgy and ritual. Little had changed even by the twelfth century, according to Rabbi Eliezer ben Yitzak, who had lived in Bohemia and Germany and who wrote in 1190 that there were no Jewish scholars in most of the Jewish communities in Hungary. Of course, the educational level among most of the Gentiles at this time was also low.

There is evidence dating from the early part of the thirteenth century that a Hungarian Jew by the name of Teha had risen to some level of prominence as financial advisor to King Endre II. Unfortunately, social pressures had begun to mount against the Jews in general and Teha in particular, and the financial advisor was obliged to leave the country sometime after 1230.

Shortly afterward, in 1241, Mongol invaders descended upon Hungary, bringing in their wake much death and destruction. The invaders were nomadic tribes that Genghis Khan had united early in the thirteenth century and who rampaged and pillaged with great speed through parts of Asia and Europe. Within a year, however, the Mongols suddenly withdrew from Hungary and other parts of Western Europe for reasons that had to do with issues of succession after the death of Ogodej Khan (third son of Genghis) in the Mongol capital some four thousand miles away. At about this time, records show that the Hungarian Jew Teha had returned home to once again act as financial advisor to the court (of King Béla IV). But as the turbulent thirteenth century drew to a close, the Jews were subjected to renewed harassment, sparked this time by the first false accusation in Hungary against a Jew for ritual murder.[2]

By the fourteenth century, the majority of Hungarian Jews were living in Pozsony, which was then the most populous town in the country. At midcentury, the reigning monarch, King Louis, seemed to be favoring the Jews, while also supporting efforts to have them converted to Christianity. Failing in this endeavor, the capricious king, in 1360, ordered their expulsion from the country. The exiles were forced to find new homes in nearby countries, with most settling in Austria and Moravia. But the absence of Jews soon deprived Hungary, and the king in particular, of much-needed financial expertise, and in 1364 the order of expulsion was reversed.

---

[1] "Magyar" describes both the alliance of nomadic tribes that conquered what would eventually become their homeland and the Hungarian language itself.

[2] Europe over the centuries would see occasional eruptions of false Christian accusations that a Jew had kidnapped a Christian for an alleged sacrifice ritual to obtain blood for the preparation of the Passover matzo, or flat bread.

Upon the return of the Jews, King Louis structured their relationship to the state with the establishment of a "national Jew judge." The post was intended to be filled by a Gentile nobleman who would not only ensure that Jews paid their especially high taxes to the royal treasury but who would also serve to protect them against hostile elements, including the Church and the townsfolk. The Church, it seems, never ceased to see Jews as killers of Christ, whereas the townspeople—mostly ethnic Germans—considered them to be dangerous competitors.

The office of national Jew judge was continued by King Sigismund in the early fifteenth century. It effectively removed administrative control over Jewish communities from the towns in which they resided, placing them directly under the jurisdiction of the crown, which continued the dual policies of heavy taxation and protection. In 1436, to further advance their social condition, Jews were accorded certain privileges in return for huge sums of money to the perpetually cash-poor King Sigismund. One such benefit allowed Jewish religious judges to render their own verdicts in cases of disputes within their own community, albeit in the presence of the Jew judge. Other privileges included the granting of royal consent to charge higher interest rates for loans made to Gentiles, as well as exemption from the higher taxes levied by the municipalities in which Jews were resident. Compared to the open and often cruel persecution faced by their brethren in neighboring countries, the Jews of Hungary appeared to be better off.

Conditions would largely remain unchanged under the reign of Hungary's great Renaissance King Mathias (1458–90). This monarch taxed all his subjects ruthlessly, but the Jews were singled out as prime targets. While not as tolerant of the community as his predecessors, there were no expulsions from the country, nor did the king allow Jews to be harmed. On the other hand, Mathias showed no such concern for the Jews in lands conquered during his reign. .

The sixteenth century was a low point in Hungarian history, following the disastrous battle of Mohacs in 1526, in which Turkish forces triumphed over the Hungarian forces. Much of the country was subjected to a prolonged occupation, and adding to the misery was a general economic decline and the opening of a major religious divide between Catholics and Protestants. Such unsettled conditions have always been dangerous for Jews, and this troubled time would see the whipping up of old hatreds, more blood libel accusations, and even expulsions from the towns of Sopron and Pozsony.

An interesting story emerged from this period about the life and times of Shneur Zalman, a Jewish convert to Christianity, who adopted the name of Imre Szerencsés, or Emericus Fortunatus. Records show that Szerencsés rose rapidly to become the most powerful financial advisor to King Louis II. Misfortune befell him, however, when he was blamed for the sorry state of the country's finances, and his house in Buda was subsequently looted and destroyed by an angry mob. Szerencsés nevertheless survived and even regained his influence. It was claimed that shortly before his death in 1526, he returned to the faith of his ancestors.

After the battle of Mohács, Jews generally fared better in areas under occupation because the Turkish authorities were indifferent to the religious practices of the local residents. As with all non-Muslims, the Jews had to pay an extra tax, but they were otherwise free to pursue their lives and their religious practices. Most notably, the Jewish community in Buda grew and prospered. In 1666, a revered rabbi, Kohen Efraim, moved from Vilna to Buda, where he gained renown as an interpreter of the Talmud.

Conditions changed again after 1686, when Buda was retaken by a Christian army. The invading force, recruited from various nationalities—mostly German- Austrians—killed many of the Turkish community in Buda, as well as a number of Jews. In their rampage, the army burned down a synagogue with its torahs and other holy books, and many Jews were taken prisoner. It required a great deal of money, donated by wealthy coreligionists from Vienna, in particular, to obtain their freedom.

Following complete liberation from the Turks in 1699, Hungarians became subjects of the Austrian Hapsburgs. Austrian and Hungarian coexistence would thereafter persevere in various forms, with only brief interruptions, until the fall of the Habsburg Monarchy in 1918.

The eighteenth century, often referred to as the Age of Enlightenment, had little impact upon the Jews of Hungary, especially during the first half of the century, when the influence of the Catholic Church was still very strong. Even during the second half, when Queen Maria Theresa embarked upon modernizing the Monarchy, she thought nothing of burdening the Jews by levying extra taxes on them. Despite such harsh economic restrictions, however, they kept coming, mainly from Austria and Moravia, and to a lesser extent from Poland. In the period between 1750 and 1800, it is estimated that the Jewish population of Hungary rose from about thirty thousand to fifty thousand.

Jews in Hungary filled niches in the society as merchants. They were valued for their economic skills, and many were encouraged to live on the estates of the great aristocratic landowners. One such haven was the town of Ó-Buda, located on the estates of the family of Count Zichy. By 1785, there were some 285 Jewish families in Ó-Buda, but by the close of the century the Jewish community had grown to become the country's largest. Meanwhile, the large towns of Buda and Pest continued to grow in importance, and they might also have attracted more Jews but for the resistance of the Gentile inhabitants.

Maria Theresa's son, Joseph II, took his mother's process of modernization to radical extremes: his overriding criterion for his subjects was loyalty to the state. In 1783, he issued an edict that considerably alleviated the social and economic pressures which had long plagued Hungary's Jews. Providing they did not harm the interests of the nobility or the privileges of the guilds, Jews were free to take up residence in the so-called "royal-free" towns. They could now rent land in these towns and take up occupations as artisans or merchants. In return, the king demanded that

Jews limit the use of the Hebrew language to liturgical ends and that they learn to write in the languages current in the society: German, Latin, Hungarian. They were also required to abandon their traditional Hebrew names and take up German ones. Court officials, who were assigned the task of giving German names to Jewish families, adopted the rather simple formula of offering names of colors: Weiss, Grün, Braun, Roth, Blau, Schwartz, etc. Positive royal initiatives opened opportunities for education and, in the 1780s, pressure was exerted upon the authorities in Buda, Pest, and Szeged to allow Jews to reside there. These changes were greeted by the Jews with general acceptance, but a decree that beards be shaved generated such heated resistance that the king felt obliged to rescind the order.

Joseph II died in 1790. Soon thereafter, a number of towns such as Pest and Nagyszombat raised demands for the expulsion of the Jews, but the appeals were all refused by the Royal Chancery. Furthermore, the Diet[3] of 1790–91, convened by reform-minded King Leopold II, confirmed the rights received earlier by the Jews. Most of the noblemen serving as delegates to this Diet were in favor of free trade—an approach shared by the Jews engaged in commerce, but opposed by the strongly conservative and privileged townspeople.

In an effort to bring some real administrative and economic reform to the country, the Diet of 1790–91 established nine committees. One of these committees discussed a renewed charge of ritual murder in Szabolcs County, and it was an aristocrat, Count József Haller, who eloquently defended the Jews: "It is absurd to think that a religion that respects God would, at the same time, commit crimes."

Unfortunately, Leopold II died in 1792, and his successor, King Francis I, was not interested in reforms, nor were most of the noblemen. Their conservatism hardened when news came of the radical turn taken by the French Revolution in the early 1790s. Shortly afterward, war would break out between Austria and revolutionary France, and fighting would continue well into the nineteenth century, when France became an empire under Napoleon.

The war years favored the merchant classes in Hungary, and this included Jewish merchants, especially those living in Pest, which had by then become an important commercial hub for Central Europe. From a total of only fourteen Jews known to be resident in Pest in 1787, the number grew to 310 by 1799.

Slowly and grudgingly, Jews came to be accepted in Hungary; but they were not yet emancipated, and they remained second-class citizens. Demands by the liberal reformers for full emancipation grew increasingly vocal by the 1830s. Their most eloquent champion was Baron

---

[3] The English translation of the Latin *Dieta*; it was a feudal assembly of estates, with the Catholic prelates and the aristocrats constituting its Upper Chamber. The noble delegates from the counties served in the Lower Chamber. Delegates from the free royal towns were also seated in the Lower Chamber, but had little influence there. The vast majority of the population—the peasants still in bondage as serfs—had no representation at all.

József Eotvos, who espoused the belief that liberty was not a reward but a right of every human being. Jews, he said, should not be condemned because they were different, as any perceived difference was not in their character but in their long suffering from the absence of freedom. At the 1840 Diet, a law was passed allowing Jews free movement in the country. This was taken as a sign that more progressive policies would be forthcoming.

However, positive attitudes could not be sustained, and this was reflected in the meetings of the Diet of 1843–45—an indication that public opinion had begun to cool somewhat towards the Jews. The mostly German townspeople were still uniformly hostile, and even some members of the nobility began to have second thoughts about their liberal positions on the issue. This shift in attitudes may have been due to the growing Jewish population: in the decade of 1840–50, their numbers increased from 244,000 to 368,000.

If there was tension at the time between Jews and non-Jews in the country, there was also a noticeable strain that had been growing between progressive Jews—those who, while retaining their religion, were willing to assimilate to a fast-developing Hungarian nation—and their Orthodox brethren, who insisted on maintaining stricter adherence to Jewish traditions.

The chief spokesperson for the progressive group was Rabbi Lipót Low of Nagykanizsa, who, in 1847, issued a manifesto and requested other rabbis to support it. A major point of this manifesto was the following declaration: "Hungary is our only country and we will do our utmost to instill love for it into the hearts of our congregations." Low's views found much favor among other rabbis and the Jews in general, and this helped to stimulate active support for ideas of Hungarian independence that flourished during the outbreak of revolution in 1848—in both Vienna and Pest

Eighteen forty-eight was the year of revolution across Europe, and the stirrings in Vienna and Pest were no exceptions. Sadly, despite the broader developments and issues engulfing Hungary during that momentous year, pogroms against Jews flared up among the townspeople in Pozsony, Nagyszombat, Szombathely, and Pest. These outpourings of hatred no doubt contributed to the decision by Lajos Kossuth—acknowledged leader of Hungarian liberals and the revolution—not to put the issue of Jewish emancipation on the legislative agenda for fear it might further fan hatred. Nevertheless, Jews joined the new Hungarian army in large numbers when the War of Independence from Austria began. According to some estimates, about twenty thousand Jews took part in the fighting. In addition, Jewish communities contributed generously to the new Hungarian state treasury; the community of Pest alone offered a considerable amount of silver and a fifty thousand forint loan.

By August 1848, a joint Austrian-Russian force defeated the Hungarians, and Austrian revenge was not long in coming, particularly against the Jews. A few rabbis were jailed, and the communities were forced to pay exorbitant sums as reparation.

After years of oppression and tentative attempts at reconciliation between Austria and Hungary, a partnership of equals was created in 1867, and a state called Austria-Hungary was formed. The new Hungarian government introduced the law of full emancipation for the Jews in the same year, and the Parliament accepted it with near-unanimous approval. Jews were now full-fledged citizens of Hungary, with all the rights of their Gentile compatriots—with one glaring omission that concerned their religion: a Jew could easily become a Christian convert, but the reverse was not sanctioned. This law was soon to be tested and overturned following a scandal in a village of Transylvania, where members of the so-called *szombatos*—or *shabbatizer*—sect wished to convert to Judaism. Overcoming protests by the Catholic Church, which tried to block the effort, Baron József Eotvos, the Minister of Culture at the time, consented to the conversion.

A Hungarian Jewish Congress was held in 1868–69, where tensions between assimilants and the Orthodox, which had simmered for years, finally burst into the open. As differences between the two camps could not be bridged, Hungarian Jewry simply split into two denominations. The assimilants, or the neolog group, favored use of the Hungarian language along with Hebrew and agreed that male and female worshippers could sit together at services. Essentially, they agreed to make accommodations to modern life. In contrast, the Orthodox community wished to keep all the Jewish traditions. To ease the assimilation of the former while preserving the essentials of Judaism, a College of Rabbinical Studies was set up, which in time became a famous center of Jewish Studies. This college was instrumental in the establishment of a rabbinate with high scholarly standards. The period of Dualism, between 1867 and 1918, was the golden age of Jews in Hungary.

There was a huge growth in numbers. In 1880, there were some 638,000 Jews in Hungary; by 1890, the figure had grown to 725,000, or 4.2 percent of the total population. The country was, at this time, experiencing a great economic boom, and the Jews came to play an extremely important role in this phenomenal development. For example, they flourished in certain professions: by 1910, Jews comprised 45.4 percent of the country's lawyers, 48.4 percent of physicians, 42.4 percent of journalists, and 37 percent of engineers, were Jewish. They also came to own many large banks and to be active in the stock market and in commerce in general. As to the field of politics, this was left, as if by some sort of silent agreement, as a monopoly of the Gentile majority. This arrangement was somewhat weakened early in the twentieth century with the emergence of the Budapest-based and heavily Jewish Democratic Party and the prominence of its leader, Vilmos Vazsonyi.

Gentile politicians clearly understood the benefits to the country of arrangements that left the Jews free to pursue their economic interests, and they were therefore adamantly opposed to any resurgence of anti-Semitism. An anti-Semitic political party had functioned in the 1880s, but lost its support in the decade that followed. Furthermore, most Jews, certainly those in the majority neolog denomination, became ardent Hungarian patriots—an important consideration in the context of the multinational mix that characterized both Austria and Hungary in different ways. In Hungary proper, Hungarians made up the largest ethnic group, but they were in the minority compared to the total number of non-Hungarians: Germans, Slovaks, Croats, Serbs, Romanians, and Ruthenians. This in turn led to a delicate ethnic balancing act as the Hungarians wished to strengthen "Magyar supremacy," the expression they often used at the time. The vast majority of Jews enthusiastically declared their loyalty to Hungary, becoming active supporters of Magyar language and culture, especially in the territories where most of the inhabitants were non-Magyars. Therefore, from the Hungarian point of view, Jews were a welcome addition to the Hungarian ranks, tipping the delicate ethnic balance in the Hungarians' favor. As a reward, in 1895, the Jewish religion was formally acknowledged as one of the country's "historic" religions. The flip side of this was the lack of popularity of Zionism—a growing Jewish nationalist movement whose aim was the establishment of a homeland for Jews in Palestine.[4]

Jews in Hungary had also become prominent in the arts and sciences. Among poets, József Kiss became very popular, while Ferenc Molnár and Menyhért Lengyel achieved fame among writers and playwrights. Béla Balázs was a well-known novelist and dramatist, and Ernö Szép gained prominence as a poet. Ignotus and Ernö Osvát were known as editors of the path-breaking literary magazine, *Nyugat*. György Lukács became a world-famous philosopher; and Gyula Pikler, Oszkár Jászi, and Ervin Szabo excelled as sociologists. Some of the outstanding high schools in Budapest produced eminent scientists, including János von Neumann, Leo Szilárd, Teodor von Kármán, Jenö Wigner, and Edward Teller—all of whom gained world renown abroad after World War II.

In World War I, Hungarian Jewish soldiers took an active part in the fighting. Many were killed or wounded, and many among the survivors returned from the battlefields to receive decorations for bravery. The pressures of the protracted war, however, produced great stress within the country, and this expressed itself openly in anti-Semitic acts. Forgetting the bravery and sacrifice of Jewish soldiers at the front, Jews in general were accused of draft-dodging and war-profiteering. The war ended in defeat, and soon Hungary became, very briefly (March 21 to August 1, 1919), a Communist regime—the only one apart from a similarly brief experiment in Munich, Germany, and, of course, Soviet Russia. The Hungarian Communist government, known by the name of its leader, or the Béla Kún regime, quickly became unpopular. Sadly, most Communist leaders, including Béla Kún himself, were Jewish, a fact that further inflamed anti-Semitism. Several Jews fell victim to the so-called White Terror that followed the fall of the

---

[4] This writer's own grandfather, born in 1868 and who lived his life as a very religious Jew, felt bound to cut all ties with a nephew who had become a Zionist.

regime in August. In the aftermath, Jews were blamed for the sins of the Béla Kún regime, even though the so-called Red Terror had previously executed forty-four Jews and kept close to one hundred in jail. In 1920, the major victors in the war—with France taking the lead—imposed an extremely punitive treaty upon Hungary. The document, known as the Treaty of Trianon, virtually dismembered the country in a catastrophic fashion. Although all Jewish organizations condemned this treaty, the pain and suffering connected to it brought forth a strong resurgence of anti-Semitic sentiment.

The new, so-called counterrevolutionary regime of Admiral Miklós Horthy began a policy of discrimination against the Jews. In 1920, the Parliament passed the Numerus Clausus, a law that curtailed the number of Jewish students admitted to universities. The severity of that law was eased somewhat by 1928, but in practice, racial and religious considerations continued to play a role in the student selection process. In the 1930s, as successive Hungarian governments closed ranks with Nazi Germany, legislators began to place increasing limitations upon the freedom of Jews to pursue educational, social, and economic opportunities. For a time, major Jewish capital interests weathered the storm better than the owners of small enterprises. After the outbreak of World War II and the entry by Hungary into Hitler's anti-Soviet campaign in 1941, Jewish males were called up and forcibly enrolled—not in the regular army, but in so-called labor battalions. The casualty rate was high among these workers. During the winter of 1942–43, there were some forty-four thousand Jewish laborers on the Eastern Front, of whom only six thousand to seven thousand survived.

The greatest calamity commenced March 19, 1944, with the German occupation of Hungary. Jews from the countryside were quickly deported, mostly to Auschwitz. Hundreds of thousands perished there and in other death camps. The Germans had also planned the deportation of the Jews of Budapest, but the head of state, Miklós Horthy, having received strong warnings from abroad, raised objections, and the mass deportation did not take place. The seizure of power by the Hungarian fascist Arrow Cross Party, on October 15, 1944, posed immediate mortal danger to the country's remaining Jews. Many were killed by Arrow Cross thugs, and only the actions of the Swiss Red Cross, a few neutral diplomatic missions, and the personal interventions of the Swiss Carl Lutz and the Swede Raoul Wallenberg, were able to save the lives of others. Hungarian Christian rescuers, including the Lutheran pastor Gábor Sztehlo, who saved this writer's life, performed personal acts of heroism by sheltering the persecuted. Surprisingly, it was a German general who stopped the plan by the Arrow Cross for the extermination of the Jews in the Budapest ghetto. All in all, about one hundred thousand Jews survived in Budapest—including seventy thousand in the ghetto and those who had remained in various houses protected by neutral countries or who had managed to hide elsewhere.

The story of Jews in postwar Hungary is beyond the scope of this brief history, and only a summary sketch can be drawn here. Following the war, Zionism gained immense popularity among the young Jewish survivors, and many soon left to begin new lives in what was then Palestine. After the 1956 revolution, there was another large exodus of Jews. Today, in the wake of the collapse of the Soviet system, anti-Semitism is still to be found in the country, and the Jewish population is obliged to deal with occasional eruptions of hatred. But official discrimination is outlawed, and Jews are not prevented from occupying prominent positions. The pace of assimilation remains high, as does the rate of intermarriage, and this may account for the large number of close relationships and friendships between Jews and non-Jews. In 2002, a Holocaust survivor, Imre Kertész, became the first Hungarian writer to receive the Nobel Prize in Literature.

GLOSSARY

- **1956 Revolution:** The popular uprising of the Hungarians against the Communist government, which was put down by the Soviet Armed Forces.

- **Admiral (Miklo's) Horthy:** Regent of Hungary from 1920 to1944. He did not protest the anti-Jewish laws, but covertly tried to join the Allies as the war seemed to be turning against Germany. He was replaced by the ruthless anti-Semitic fascist dictator, Szálasi, in 1944.

- **Air raid shelter:** A designated shelter during bombardments.

- **American PX:** The shop where the American army could procure American goods in foreign countries.

- **Arrow Cross (*Nyilas*):** Hungarian National Socialist Party founded in 1937 by Ferenc Szálasi. It assumed power in October 1944 and was responsible for the mass murder of Hungarian Jews until the Russian Liberation in January 1945. They wore armbands with the insignia of two intersecting arrows.

- **Auschwitz:** The largest and most notorious annihilation camp in the German concentration camp network, located in Poland. It was the final destination of most of the Hungarian Jews.

- **Beads:** Beads used in counting prayers (especially Catholic rosary).

- **Bergen-Belsen:** A notorious concentration camp in Germany, where many Hungarian Jews were transported and many perished.

- **Blood for Trucks**. Adolf Eichmann presented the Relief and Rescue Committee of Budapest with an offer that would be known as "Blood for Trucks," in which Eichmann would barter "a million Jews" for goods obtained outside of Hungary, including ten thousand trucks for civilian use, or, as an alternative, for use on the eastern front. The rescue scheme was never implemented.

- **Bomb shelter:** (see **Air raid shelter**)

- **Brick Factory:** (*Téglagyár* in Hungarian) An open-air collection center in a former brick factory outside Budapest, used as a departure point for Jews to be deported to concentration camps.

- **British Mandate:** After the dissolution of the Ottoman Empire at the end of World War I, the League of Nations gave Great Britain the mandate to administer territories in the Middle East, which included present day Israel, then called Palestine.

- **Bunker:** (see **Air raid shelter**)

- **Cattle cars:** The wagons of the trains, normally used to transport cattle, in which Jewish deportees were taken to the concentration camps. Occupants were crowded into the small space without food or water, sometimes for days of travel.

- **Coal cellar:** A space in the basement of a building where coal was stored for heating. In some houses, these served as bomb shelters or places of refuge of hidden Jews. In many of the apartment buildings in Budapest, each apartment was assigned its own enclosed storage space.

- **Collection camp (center):** A place where deportees were held until their deportation to a final destination, such as a concentration camp.

- **Comb-out:** (see *Razzia)*

- **Concentration camp:** One of the notorious centers, most of them in Germany or Poland, where Jews and other "undesirables" were deported, housed in lagers in tiered bunks, fed starvation rations, often made to work at excruciating tasks or submitted to medical experiments and, in the case of the annihilation camps, gassed and cremated, sometimes on arrival.

- *Csendör:* A Hungarian gendarme, a member of the police in districts across the country outside Budapest. They were often used to execute the orders leading to the incarceration and deportation of the Jews.

- **Death Marches:** Forced marches of prisoners over long distances and under intolerable conditions was another way victims of the Third Reich were killed. The prisoners, guarded heavily, were treated brutally, and many died from mistreatment or were shot. Prisoners were transferred from one ghetto or concentration camp to another ghetto or concentration camp or to a death camp.
  Some historians, however, claim only those marches that took prisoners directly to be killed were "Death Marches", as opposed to "Forced Marches".

- **Deportation:** The transporting of Jews from their homes to concentration camps in cattle cars.

- **Dohány utca Synagogue:** The main synagogue in Budapest and the largest in Europe, recently restored.

- **DP (Displaced Person):** At the end of World War II in Europe, millions of people lived involuntarily in places other than the homes they had occupied before the war. Some tried to return, while others waited for an opportunity to immigrate to countries like Canada, the United States, or Palestine.

- **DP Camp:** At the end of World War II, DP camps were established until the inhabitants, the persons displaced by the war, found a permanent home.

- *Dunapart:* The bank of the Danube in Budapest. For the purpose of these stories, it signifies the place of execution of Jews trapped by the SS or the Hungarian *Nyilas*. The victims were lined up on the banks of the almost completely frozen river and shot into the water among the ice floes. Often three were tied together and only one was shot, dragging the other two with him into the water to drown.

- **Eastern Front:** The battlegrounds in Russia and the Ukraine, where the Russian army fought the invading Germans. Many Jewish Hungarian men, who were conscripted for forced labor (*munkaszolgálat*), were taken there to support the troops as noncombatants. Only a few returned after the war.

- **False papers (documents):** The forged or "borrowed" birth, marriage, and baptismal certificates that conferred on the Jewish bearer a false Christian identity.

- **Final Solution:** Hitler's plan to exterminate all the Jews.

- **Forced labor:** The conscription of Jewish Hungarian males to do work to support the Hungarian and German troops as noncombatants. Sometimes this work was in Hungary and of temporary nature, often outside the country, as on the Eastern Front, from where many never returned.

- **Freedom fighter:** A participant in the Hungarian Revolution of 1956.

- **German Occupation of Hungary:** The period from March 19, 1944, until the Russian Liberation of the country in the winter of 1945; the period when the German army occupied Hungary and enforced the Jewish Laws leading to the Final Solution.

- *Gimnázium*: Secondary school in Hungary with an academic curriculum, consisting of eight grades, from fifth (first) to twelfth (eighth) grade.

- *Hachshara* (**Hebrew**): A preparation, usually for agricultural work before settlement in Palestine.

- **Hidden Children:** Jewish children who had false papers testifying to their Christian identity or were hiding without documents.

- **Horthy, Miklos:** (see **Admiral (Miklo's) Horthy**)

- **Hungarian Revolution:** (see **1956 Revolution**)

- **Internment camp:** A collection place for those deported from their homes, usually on the way to a concentration camp.

- **Iron Guard:** Ultranationalist, anti-Semitic, anti-Hungarian legionnaires in Romania.

- **Jewish Ghetto:** The part of a city where all the Jews were obliged to live under strict surveillance and curfew. They were identified by the wearing of the yellow star. The inhabitants of the ghetto were crowded, with many families sharing an apartment and living in constant fear of deportation or of being taken to the Dunapart to be shot.

- **Jewish House:** A building outside of the ghetto where Jews were obliged to live before the establishment of the ghetto. These buildings were identified by a yellow star.

- **Jewish Laws:** The collection of regulations that the Jews had to observe, including the wearing of the yellow star, observing a curfew, moving into the ghetto, losing their businesses, and being excluded from activities such as schooling and the fabric of the normal life of a citizen.

- **JOINT (Jewish American Distribution Committee):** During the war this organization helped Jews escape and find shelters in safe countries. After the war it helped Jews who were in DP camps, and it continued to be instrumental in helping resettlement and establishing orphanages.

- *Judenrein* **(German):** Literally meaning "cleansed of Jews."

- *Kaddish:* The ritual Jewish prayer to commemorate the dead.

- *L'chaim:* The Hebrew toast meaning "to life."

- *Lager:* The building that housed the inmates of a concentration camp.

- **Liberation:** The arrival of the victorious Soviet forces in Hungary in the winter of 1945, signaling the defeat of the German army and the end of the German Occupation. Often, this meant further hardships for the emaciated and traumatized citizens, in spite of their relief at being liberated. Different parts of Hungary were liberated at different times. The western part was the last. Fighting there extended into April 1945.

- **March 19, 1944:** The beginning of the German Occupation of Hungary.

- **Mauthausen:** One of the notorious German concentration camps, located in Austria.

- *Mikéfe:* The acronym of *Magyar Izraelita Kézmüves és Földmüvelési Egyesület*. It is an association of Hungarian Jews that sponsored an agricultural school in Budapest to train Jews to be farmers.

- *Munkaszolgálat:* (see **Forced labor**)

- **Neolog:** Conservative Jews, as opposed to Orthodox.

- *Nyilas:* (see **Arrow Cross**)

- **Orthodox Jew:** A Jewish individual who adheres strictly to the Jewish religious laws.

- **Palestine:** (see **British Mandate**)

- **Protected House:** A building in which Jews were supposedly protected by a foreign government that was neutral in World War II. The inhabitants of these buildings carried documents in their own name testifying to the protection of these countries' embassies. Switzerland, Sweden, and Spain were some of the countries offering this protection. Toward the end of the war, this protection was often not honored.

- **Protection of consulate (Swiss, Swedish, Spanish, etc...) :** (see **Protected House**)

- **Ration cards:** The cards issued to each individual, which could be exchanged for staples like sugar, flour and milk, without which it was impossible to buy provisions except on the black market during the time of extreme shortages.

- *Razzia:* A search in a certain area for some individuals, during which time the area was cordoned off, restricting access and exit.

- **Regent of Hungary:** (see **Admiral (Miklós) Horthy**)

- **Resistance (Dutch, Zionist, French):** The movements organized to defy the German authority, usually composed of individuals who risked their lives to save others, such as rescuing and hiding Jews.

- *Rosh Hakal:* The president of a Jewish community.

- **Russian Front:** (see **Eastern Front**)

- **Russian Liberation:** (see **Liberation**)

- **Safe House :** (see **Protected House**)

- **Szálasi, *Ferenc*:** Leading figure of Hungarian Nazism. He headed the extremist Arrow Cross (*Nyilas*) party. In 1944, he became new head of State of Hungary, ruling the Jews with terror and cruelty. In1945, he fled the liberated city, but was captured and found guilty by the People's Tribunal of war crimes, and was executed.

- **Selection in Auschwitz:** The procedure that determined whether the Jews arriving at the camp would be immediately sent to the gas chamber or allowed to remain alive to be put to work, or sometimes serve as objects of medical experiments.

- *Siddur:* A Jewish prayer book.

- **Siege of Budapest:** The approximately one hundred days during the winter of 1944/45 while the Soviet army and the German and Hungarian forces carried on their combat for Budapest. Fortunately for the Jews remaining in Budapest, it was the Russians who were victorious.

- **SS (*Schutzstaffel*):** The "protective detachment" founded in 1925 as Hitler's bodyguard. From the initial few hundred troops, it had expanded to two hundred thousand by the 1930s. The SS assumed the responsibility for the Final Solution and ran the camps.

- **Star house:** (see **Jewish House**)

- **Strawman:** A non-Jew willing to administer a business owned by a Jew, pretending to own it in order to save the business for the Jewish owner.

- *Téglagyár:* (See **Brick Factory**)

- **The Righteous:** Individuals honored officially by Israel who, at the risk of their own lives, helped Jews survive the Holocaust.

- **Theresienstadt:** One of the notorious concentration camps, located in Bohemia (Czechoslovakia). It was falsely designated as a "show place" to assure the Red Cross that Jews were not being mistreated there, while in reality the inhabitants were gradually being sent in increments to the death camps for annihilation.

- *Védett Ház:* (see **Safe House**)

- *Wehrmacht*: The German army, which was falsely purported not to be involved in the Final Solution.

- **White star:** The designated insignia to be worn by converted Jews. This was erroneously thought to protect the bearers from the same treatment as the wearers of the Yellow Star.

- *Yad Vashem*: The Holocaust Martyrs' and Heroes' Remembrance Authority in Jerusalem established by the Israeli government to house the Holocaust archives, a museum, and a memorial to honor the Righteous.

- **Yellow Star:** (see **Jewish Star**)

- **Yellow Star House:** (see **Jewish House**)

"Garden of Dohány Street Synagogue, Budapest"

There is a willow tree in the garden
Made of stone and steel forged by man,
Firmly rooted in the earth of this holy place,
A memorial.

The branches gently sway in the breeze,
Leaves engraved with names whisper of lives
Snuffed out by scorching breaths of hate.
This willow will never wilt or die.
It will withstand the test of time telling tales of
Young and Old burned in fires,
Drowned in torrents of hate. As the world
Stood still in the rivers of tears.

So when you gaze at the willow tree
In this garden of prayer do not weep!
Remember and hold dear their memories
As only You, the forever surviving Jew can do!

Miriam Steinmetz, 2008